PIG SNORT

GW00692262

PIG SNORT

Reg Carr

The
Halcyon
Press

Published by

The Halcyon Press

A division of

Halcyon Publishing Ltd

P.O. Box 360, Auckland, New Zealand

Printed by
Prolong Press Ltd
China

ISBN 978-1-877256-88-2

Contents

INTRODUCTION

Now that I've finished writing the book perhaps I'd better start on the introduction bit. I know it's back-to-front – I just started writing the stories and got carried away. Besides, I might have got half way through and given up, and then any introduction would have been a waste of time.

And that's the reason I write anyway. I'm remembering back to when it all happened and am trying to recapture the buzz it brings and the excitement we had at the time. I get almost as much fun out of retelling the chase as I did when it happened, but feel this book will be my "swan-song," or "pig snort," if you like. Likely, it will be my last major effort so I sincerely hope that you will enjoy what's written.

I know that when Sam and Kalvin read what happened they'll realise I have made a mistake or two – not intentional believe me, but all put together the way my memory serves me and for the fun of it.

I've had the help of a great team of women, all family, this time around. It's all very well to scribble longhand some 70-80 thousand words, but quite different having to decipher all that and type it into a computer or laptop. I'm hopeless on a laptop, though I've got one now, and have had to ask for help from my girls who are far more literate on these things than I'll ever be. They all came through marvellously for me and I'm indebted to, and humbled by them for their response and willing help.

Daughters Sharon Ackers and Angela Carr did I don't know how many thousands of words for me, as did grandaughters Tamzin Ackers and Rebekah and Jamie-Lee Wilkie. It's boring work I guess, tapping away for hours when you're not really into the hunting scene but they did it all for their dad or grandad. Thank you truly to you five lasses!

The whanau at Lincoln, and Emma's wedding, nine hunters here.

To my wonderful grandaughter-in-law Roxanne Harrison I owe a special and very big thank you. She only lives a few kilometres away and has been plagued at all hours with dumb-fool questions and has always responded most graciously –"Roxy, the screens gone blank, what do I do now?"– "I can't get the cursor to drop down any more"–"How do I get out of this stupid box that's appeared on the thing?" etc. Then she's been around to arrange MY laptop into some sort of order, and printed off heaps of pages too. Thanks a million Roxy!

Those printed-off pages I had to go through and check for mistakes due to my indecipherable longhand; and I did get some good laughs. Out-found became out-bound, parentage was put as percentage, imitating turned into initiating, something downed instead of dawned on us, and Whippet cross dogs were "mire" streamlined than – Yeah, that part of it was a lot of fun!

And I've been able to twist my work-mate's arm so that he produced a few splendidly done cartoons (he's never seen me naked and is only guessing there), but a big thanks to Mark Tyree of Kerikeri.

I don't know how many months or years I'll carry on with my own dogs. I fear they don't get enough practice these days, but are still going well. One day I'll decide to sell them and be content to go visit Peter Greenhill and reminisce about the good old days when we hunted together. Or go out with Sam Harris, Kalvin Roycroft and others, for at 66 (and counting) after having had a stroke I really don't know what's around the corner. Olive reckons I'm grumpy, I disagree. Maybe a tad grouchy, but definitely not grumpy! But now that the book-writing is over I may relax (deadlines – you know) and take her out more, fatten her up and make her more cuddly. I reckon we should all treat our women like we treat our dogs (mine [the dogs] certainly aren't skinny). Or treat our dogs like we treat our women. They're both pretty good, loyal and loving aren't they! I'm the "alpha male" at my place, but at times, just now and again, it's good to pretend otherwise eh!

And as parting advice? Have a care for the piggie-wiggies too. Treat them humanely where you can. It's not always easy I know, but where you can.

Just now the news on "tele" is of the flooding in Myanmar and the earthquake in China. I look back on 37 years of hunting, and my life in general, and must acknowledge like King David did in the Psalms "The lines are fallen to me in pleasant places, yea I have a goodly heritage." Old-fashioned grammar for sure but how accurately it describes you and me, our lot in life. I've had a fantastic time hunting and would dearly love to carry on. But who knows? Someone up above does and I confidently leave myself in His hands. Be encouraged to do the same for you won't be disappointed.

I'm supposed to be going hunting with Kalvin in the morning but it's raining heavy and I'm trying to think of an excuse to stay home. Well, not really, though I do hope the rain stops. We're going to catch a big broken-coloured boar regardless. I can feel it in my bones. We're going to chase him anyway, off his ridge and into the gully where – It's great fun eh. Go for it, and I wish you luck.

God bless you (as He has).

Regards,

Reg

Benji Or Too Many Cooks

Bumped into Marty Briscoe outside Mitre 10 on Thursday last week and got yakking about the usual – weather, kids, lamb prices, hunting and so on. The sun was steaming the countryside after yesterday's continuous rain, but seeing it was winter, didn't get too much attention in the conversation. And I already knew his youngest daughter was away for the weekend, downcountry somewhere visiting family so didn't dwell on that either (his wife Gwen had passed on nearly three years ago now and Marty didn't like talking about it, so avoided that as well). Lamb prices? Not worth a mention really, though we did touch on it half-pie, sort of!

"Might as well turn them all out in the bush for all we're getting for them," he grumbled. "They'd be easier to catch than that confounded boar we've been after."

"Yeah! I hear Kenny Montieth had it bailed up pretty good last weekend too!"

"Kenny Montieth! Couldn't catch a cold in a b____ dungeon. He's full of bullshit! Probably didn't even find the b____ thing!"

I knew Marty and Kenny had fallen out some time back. Something to do with Kenny hunting Marty's back paddock, the same weekend that eleven of his lambs were found dead down along the bottom fence.

Kenny avowed and declared he'd been there late on the Sunday evening – long after Marty had discovered his loss – Marty wasn't convinced.

"Those b____ meat-head dogs of his aren't under any sort of control at any time, let alone when they're out in the scrub. You just wait and see. It'll happen again sooner or later; but it wont be on my b____ place."

I thought it best to change the subject. "You wouldn't mind if my brother-in-law Trevor had a go at that pig sometime though Marty? His new dog doesn't miss much these days – just might do the trick for you."

"No! No! Trev's ok. That way at least I'd know who was on for sure. All them other dumb bastards sneak in the back way – them and their useless mutts. But I don't reckon anybody'll ever catch that one. It's five years now since I first ran him; and that's it. He just keeps running and running. Everybody's tried I guess by now and he's still there."

"I know. Randy Morgan and Kia Brass came up from the Waikato recently I hear. Didn't do any good either."

Marty laughed. "Yeah! They went back with their tails fair between their legs I reckon. It killed two dogs and cost them over $800 for two others, and never even saw it. He reckons he got close though, no more'n a mile. Tell Trevor there's a dozen in it for him if he can get it – might spur him on."

I had to laugh too. But I felt sorry for Kia and Randy. They were reputed to have about as good a team as you'd get anywhere. They featured regularly too in the more southern pig hunting competitions, which bespoke volumes. "The proof of the pudding is in the eating," it's said. Likewise, the proof of the pig dogs is in their (frequent) catching. It was obvious to anyone who thought about it and did the sums, those dogs of the Morgan/Brass pack were pretty top-notch. So to outdo that lot this pig just had to be formidable indeed. He was too, and his infamy had spread pretty far afield it seemed. Kia and Randy were coming back in a month's time, with Kia's cousin from Taihape with even more "top-notch" bailing dogs, and were reasonably optimistic of their chances.

By now all the locals had tried and failed. Bert Ludgrove from behind Kaikohe had had a go, Sam Crickle too, and Fergus McKenzie, Harry Spink, Rua Parkin, Jim Te Huna, Boss Atwood, Spur Purdy – everybody. And still the pig ran.

I hadn't yet – but wanted to. My dogs weren't super-good at this stage, and anyway, Oakura was Trev's stamping ground and I didn't feel like homing in on his patch without an invite. I had hunted with both Trevor and Andrew, his older brother on a few occasions but generally stayed further north. Andrew had died a while ago and Trevor hunted mainly with Colin Aikin these days, well, those days. Colin had recently gone to the big hunting ground in the sky too, and Trevor was on his own again. I waited, knowing an invite would come sooner or later. Yet just now Trevor was a bit cool about that. He had a new dog which was performing, or starting to perform wonders, and he didn't want to include other dogs in the pack until he was sure "Ben" had perfected his knack and settled down to a consistent rigmarole. From what

Heather told Olive, this rigmarole as Trevor called it, was going pretty good already, and Benji had nailed three good boars last month in just three hunts, and a fortnight ago got two over 130lb on the Saturday and another ninety-nine pounder on Sunday. Then on Thursday I'd just been around to Trevor and Heather's, and he'd shown me a photo taken exactly five days previously, on the Saturday, of a huge boar, caught by Benji at Mokau. It was ginger and black, weighing a monstrous 293lbs.

"Is it that one that lives behind Marty's place d'you reckon Trev?"

"Well, 'dunno! Could be. It's really just over the hill from Oakura. Time will tell I guess."

Time did tell too. Sparrow (we all just know him as Sparrow – not Sparrow something – just Sparrow) was up there on Sunday, early-like, and his dogs were onto something not too far away. Then a fine bail started up a hundred metres below him in really thick manuka and Sparrow was about to head down when all went quiet. He waited, holding his breath, then thought to step behind a small totara tree, just in case. Something blimmin' big was coming uphill towards him, and snorting like a mad bull. Had to be a pig though! Had to be the pig! Not continuous, just every few seconds, a deep grunt and a snort, then a blow and silence again a few more seconds. The barking had faded away and all he heard was the crackling of the ti-tree and fern as the animal approached. Then out it stepped, a gigantic ginger and black boar with small ears tucked back. and bristly tail swishing back and forth. Almost hairless it was, froth or saliva dripping from big ivory tusks every now and again, and making a new sort of noise. Sparrow was well up the totara tree, his dogs nowhere to be seen and the huge boar growled, a continuous low rumble in it's throat as it stared about. And this pig was peculiar. A small ginger patch covered it's left eye while a larger ginger patch covered the right. The only other ginger on the otherwise grey/black hide was another gingery/orange rectangle at the base of it's tail and extending down the scrotum and inside of it's back legs. It stood half a minute and sauntered off uphill still growling, and was last heard pushing through the old fence at the top of the ridge.

Sparrow stayed put and peered down at his three dogs who had come to sit under his tree the moment Mr Boar had moved away. Undoubtedly they had watched too – and waited! Sparrow was trying to believe what he had seen. His dogs demoralised and anxious to keep away, and an enormous pig that had to weigh 400? 500? 600lb? He couldn't decide and stayed put another hour. Then another half hour – just in case. Not long before midday he cautiously descended, picked up his rifle and snuck quickly and quietly away, straight towards the road with his dogs almost tripping him up.

That was the last time he was going to hunt there he reckoned. It just wasn't worth it!

Sparrow told Rua, Rua told Bert, Bert told Fergus and Sam, and Harry Spink. And Harry just happened to be on the phone a minute later and was telling Spur, who related it to Jim Te Huna. Boss Atwood and all the others knew within the hour and the stakes went up again. The chances of catching such a pig were negligible most reckoned, though there were a few takers.

It was discussed at Pig Hunting Club meetings and wagers were made – and cancelled – and made again later in the evening.

Seg and I heard too. Seg wanted to head down and try with his Fly. Now this dog was a smallish bitch, a black Kelpie, and had developed a knack of stopping big pigs all by herself. I had seen her at work and acknowledged that she was good all right. But against a 400lb monster?

Not a hard dog at all, but with an excellent nose, she'd drift off by herself when the other dogs were away and it wouldn't be long before she'd bark. Generally it was a good way away for had it been otherwise, other competent finders would have snuffed up it's scent and gone searching. But it wasn't for her distant finding ability that Seg prized her so highly. Rather, it was her subsequent action – or lack of it that made her such a God-send. I had seen the same sort of thing umpteen times myself and knew well the reasoning behind a boar's swift and instant flight as more aggressive dogs were heard on the trail.

Fly would find all right but never push her affront of the pig. Usually it was about ten paces off that she'd stand and challenge. And even that was not seemingly antagonistic. It was more an "I've seen you piggy, don't be alarmed" sort of voice. And too often for their own good, piggys would lift their heads or stand on their feet and look over at the dog. It didn't seem to be doing much, not pushing onto their patch, no in-their-face belligerence being thrown at them, and so, not feeling greatly threatened, would simply raise their hackles and keep a weather-eye on the black Kelpie

But this is what Seg listened for, her homely intermittent "yak, yak."

"Howdy pig! Howdy again!"

This would continue a couple of hours, and if Seg didn't arrive and shoot the pig Fly would be back with him, or home by nightfall. And

14

generally, if the other dogs heard, they'd home in and inevitably scare the brute into a run. Sometimes his stopping dog (not Fly) would sit the pig down and allow Rough or Pluto to catch his ears. The rest you know.

"We should go down with just Fly eh Reg? We'd stand a pretty good chance don't you think?"

I thought of Flash and Doon and Snow, the fun they would have but they were young at this stage and still not really doing it, and knew it wasn't really their scene anyway yet.

"Righto. I'll ring Marty and see if I can jack it up for Saturday. Sure worth a try."

Early on the appointed day Seg and I left the Land-Rover at Marty's main gate and hoofed it with Fly and a rifle each to the back of the farm. It was bitterly cold and our hands were deep in our pockets as we scanned the new countryside about us. The piercing wind blew along behind and had us frowning in irritation as soon as we stepped out of the vehicle.

"You had a shower recently Seg? We don't want the thing to get wind of us before we start eh!"

"Didn't think it'd matter with you along mate. Your aversion to soap and water assures us an aroma that – 'Gag!' -' Gag!' Ah. Forget it!"

I sniffed and stopped dead.

"You didn't did you?"

"What? Do what?"

"Drop your guts or some-such?"

"Na, I thought it was you!"

I glanced around some more. We had stopped and both knew in spite of our ragging each other that there was something dead not too far away.

"Look over behind that poplar," this from Seg, pointing ahead on our left.

Where the creek ran out of the left-hand valley and emptied onto the plain, or flatter ground, a "poly" cow had rolled over and stuck her four legs in the air. The blowflies knew that signal and now it was a seething mass of white crawly things. We angled over to have a look and were galvanised by the huge hoof-prints all around. "His" were the only marks seeable and we looked in awe at the proof of just how big this here quarry really was. "I reckon we should go home mate" I said to Seg, glancing nervously at the gully ahead of us.

"But Fly will warn us Reg. Don't worry, stick with me. We're here now so may as well have a go. C'mon, it's only a pig."

"A "big" pig mate," I managed to squeak. "You go in front."

"OK. You make sure you come too though."

We ventured off towards the left-hand gully, and picked up the boar's marks heading the same way just as we got to the bush edge. Kanuka and kahikatea grew in great profusion at the foot of the hills on each side of the creek but gave way to more solid puriri, rimu and taraire. As the bush ascended the ridges, various shades of dark green, so peaceful and pleasing to the eye, mottled the slopes away above and in front, and being so quiet you never knew just what might be up ahead.

"I think-".

"No you don't."

"I really do think we should wait here Seg. Fly should find it from here," I said gazing at the brooding forest ahead of us. "It won't have gone too far after a big feed of beef like that – don't you think?"

"Probably gone well back to rest up – too far for Fly yet. We'll carry on a wee way yet I reckon."

More nervous than ever (it was all right for Cedric – he hadn't seen the photo of Trevor's big pig – supposedly smaller than the "monster') I kept close to my mate and peeked over his shoulder when I could.

An hour had gone by, the sun was out getting hotter on the minute though beneath the canopy we were okay that-a-way, and the breeze was still coming from behind. Fly worked assiduously and wasn't too often at heel, ferreting out all sorts of scents and odours. She came just now and looked up at Cedric, seemingly quite earnestly and padded off straight uphill.

"Somethings up Reg," he whispered.

"Eh? What you reckon?"

"Sh!"

"Where?" (quietly)

"Dunno, Somewhere though."

We waited, me crouched down a bit behind Fleming. Then a long way off Fly barked, just once. A half minute later there was a very faint sound off in the distance, hard to decipher. There was no way really of telling what it was but Seg suddenly reckoned he knew what was up.

That's that pig Reg, comin' towards us flat out. We'd better get out of _____."

I never heard the "here." He was gone. Me too, that instant, but I was behind. Now I can run pretty fast. Won all my races at school I did. (Somewhere in the middle of the pack), but I couldn't catch Seg. No way! He was looping and leaping and jumping and racing, zooming as fast as he knew how for the sunshine and wide open spaces. (You'd never get a chance for a shot in the bush he explained later – better where you can track him, lead a bit and get a clear shot away – you know).

Extra good thinking I thought at the time. We burst out of the bush gasping and sucking in great lungsful of air, and shot right out into the middle of the paddock before looking over our shoulder. No pig in sight yet. Good!

Seg looked at the ground, puffed a bit, said rather sheepishly "might pay to load your gun Reg – just in case."

"Yeah mate, too right." I busied myself with that chore as I sized up the distance to the gate and Seg's Land-Rover.

But nothing happened. Fly arrived quite unconcernedly pretty well about then and we decided the pig must have been too far away to find after all – but we had tried hadn't we.

"Too right mate. We gave it a good go."

"May as well call round and tell Marty and say thanks I suggested whereupon we curtailed our hunting for the day and popped in at Marty's place bang on 11am. He was heading to the house and invited us in for a "cuppa" and so's we could tell him all about where we'd been and what we saw etc.

So that's what we did. Beautiful hot tea, gingernuts dipped in it too, and even some scones he warmed up in the microwave. Them with melted butter and jam on were enough to loosen our tongues and tell him of the miles we had walked – must have got near over to PuhiPuhi Road, the one 100 pounder we'd caught too far back to bring out (hadn't even thought to cut off it's tail to show him) "Na, we're more into trophy jaws you know, big tusks – that sort of thing."

He nodded and nodded and kept a very straight face. "See anybody else?"

"Not a soul mate – had the bush to ourselves."

"That's funny, Graeme Dunn called in an hour ago and reckoned he saw a coupla blokes with guns bolt out of the bush near your vehicle. He was fencing up on his back hill and watched a while. They didn't go near your Land-Rover though while he was watching."

Seg's face was a bright pink. Marty was looking at me fortunately, and I just gulped twice and stammered. "Heck, I hope we haven't lost anything out of the truck. Poaching blighters might have took anything!"

"Yeah – anything," agreed Marty.

About then a blue Hilux, pulled up at the gate and a bloke marched up the driveway and knocked on the door.

"Morning Marty, how's things?"

"Good Trevor, good. Yourself?"

"Pretty good too mate, pretty good."

"Well, come on in and have a cup of tea while it's hot. Meet Reg and Sig– Sag– – Sug — what's your name again mate?

"Seg," says Trevor. Was Sed, short for Cedric but it got changed. Seg – has been for a long time now – eh Seg!"

"Yeah Trev. Good to see you. But what are you doing here at midday?"

"Oh, I've just come for my dozen."

There was dead silence.

"You mean you've got it Trev?" An incredulous note was in even Marty's voice as he asked the question. "I don't believe it."

"You will when you see it. You and Reg and Seg can come and give me a hand to drag it out. It's really only about 50 metres off the grass at the bottom of the other gully. Hadn't hardly got started when Ben shot off uphill and bailed pretty well straight off. I just snuck in and shot it."

"When was this?"

"You fellows had just hopped in your truck when Ben found it. You were gone before I was able to sneak in and get a shot away."

Seg and I both looked out of the window at the same time, then glanced at the ceiling simultaneously. Marty was quick then with "Righto then lads, lets have a look before I part with my beer."

Before we all hopped in Trevor's double cab, I spied this queer-looking dog on the back, tied with a short rope and lying on an old sack.

"Whatever on earth is that Trevor?," I asked with by mouth open.

"Oh, that's Ben."

"That?"

"Yep, that's him."

"Cor blimey – poor dog."

"Poor pig you mean."

Here was a dog what seemed to have a permanent scowl, its face sort of puckered up and it's tail curled tightly over it's back. It was tan and white, and on second thoughts it may have been permanently grinning. It was different – now there's a good word. Different!!!

It looks like Benji's pig – but it's actually Sam's 150lber.

Twenty minutes later we were looking at a different sight again. Not far above the bush edge, in relatively open scrub and on a small flat piece of ground lay an enormous grey/black pig with three gingery/brown patches on him. And tusks like an elephant's. My guess went to a weight of 400lb. Seg reckoned 450 and Marty surmised around 450 plus, maybe quite a bit more. Trevor swore we were all wrong – and too heavy. "Be under 300lb." It turned out to be 371lb – definitely the one Sparrow saw, gingery patches, bald, and certainly the runner no one else could catch.

"How did you catch it Trev?" Seg finally got out.

"Just shot it. See, here?"

"Yeah, but how?"

"Ben just bailed it for me. It wasn't going anywhere, wasn't fazed at all apparently. Never even saw me."

"Yeah, but how?"

"Well you've got to know your dog of course. Ben shot away pretty worked up I could tell, and bailed straight off about 15 metres distant. He just gave off a faint "Yip", if you could call it that. The pig just stood up and looked at him. I snuck in – course you can see it's pretty open here."

"Wasn't he going to town, you know, barking and yapping his head off?"

"No, he can't bark. He's a Basenji – hardly any voice. The pig doesn't feel threatened, and I've no other dogs to freak it out – piece of cake."

"Where do you get them dogs?" Seg, Marty and I all looked at one another as we all spoke the same thing. Trevor just tapped the side of his nose and grinned knowingly.

Don Quixote Rides Again

"It's more blessed to give than receive" is an old maxim first spoken by Jesus and one that remains very true today. The smile on the face of a birthday present recipient is truly beyond price, indeed anything given brings it's own reward. A warm glow within is sometimes all one gets and I set out one day hunting and ended up with only that, but it was certainly worth it.

My friend Ian McDonald often had overseas vacationers stay at his place. His daughter Carol and son-in-law Roy were in charge of a Christian Youth Camp – come horse-ranch downcountry and were rarely without itinerant overseas workers. Young folk would come and spend time helping out and move on after their stint of service expired. Carol would recommend her dad as someone to go and see up in the far north and so they would arrive. Ian introduced me one day to a chap from Germany who thought he'd like to try pig hunting while in New Zealand. His English was pretty good really compared with some Germans I have heard. A few years previous to this on a terribly wet and windy night we heard a knock on the back door and I went to see a young couple standing on the doorstep, sheltering out of the rain and looking pretty bedraggled and miserable. The man spoke hesitantly.

"You not mind we sleep your shed? Please? We pay. We be no trouble. Just sleep."

She was somewhere around 25-30 years old and rather pretty. He was maybe a little older and added pleadingly, "My wife, she cold, tired. We come Paihia, but fine when we leave. We have own food, we – ."

"Come inside man, come on," I said to him and stood back. Olive had overheard it all and came to the door to add her welcome. Their packs were left in the porch and inside they came to huddle beside the heater as Olive heated up some soup and made a cup of tea. They really were grateful and after a while had thawed out considerably.

Over the meal I told him I was a hunter, and that later if the rain lifted, I was going to go hunting, looking for a big boar I was currently chasing at the coast property of a friend of the family.

They both pricked up their ears so to speak and asked embarrassedly if they could tag along. His English was really quite reasonable and I could understand most of what he said, but her's was pretty hopeless and she often lapsed back into German, appealing to him to tell me what she was trying to say.

He particularly wanted to be able to take photos of New Zealand wildlife as he was sub-editor or some-such of a magazine based not far from Frankfurt. This magazine featured wild animals from all over the world, and while he wasn't here primarily on a picture gathering exercise, this was too good an opportunity to pass up.

We yarned a good deal, poring over a map of Germany and having a good time. Olive and his wife (whose name I have forgotten, but will call her Miriam – it's written down with their address somewhere) got up and did the dishes while he and I went outside and checked the weather. A full moon was high up by now and the clouds had well nigh all gone though the wind was still stiff and fairly cool. But with my "Swanni" on and Eric in my heavy jacket I reckoned we'd be okay. Miriam was to wear a thick woollen overcoat (lent her by Olive) and her gumboots and appeared pretty excited.

We had browsed through a few editions of the *NZ Pighunter* and looked at *Diary of a Pig Hunter* by that Carr fellow and were quite hyped-up by the time we finally set off in the Land Rover.

The rest of the story is told in *The Boar and the Pig Dog* in the chapter called "The Runner", on pages 199-200. Basically, we saw the boar, but missed out on catching it, never did in fact. What's more, I missed out on the magazine Eric promised to send me and guessed he had either misplaced my address, or the thing had gone missing on it's way from Germany. Too bad. Perhaps he thought my dogs were useless and it was a case of "no hog –no mag".

This latest chap Marcus had rather a good grasp of our language and was even better than Eric. So on a lovely fine day with a little bit of wind from the west, we gathered up the dogs and the necessary gear and went walkabout from Stuart's woolshed.

The long open grassy ridges gave way in the gullies to gorse and these often harboured the wild pigs. Today though we steered well clear of the gullies as I intended to look at a patch of scrub that covered about a hundred acres a fair way further back than I usually went.

A deep raupo-infested swamp wound around the foot of three ridges and ended up flowing as a metre-wide creek under some tall old pine trees, then backwards and forwards through a gorse covered flat. The ridges still retained plenty of manuka and fern but as usual had quite an infestation of gorse as well. Quite a few totara trees grew on one part of the hillside, though these weren't very big as yet. They were dwarfed anyway by the very old and very tall radiata pine trees parked along the boundary fence, and the whole place was sort of off the beaten track and didn't get hammered by the local hunters too much. I intended to check out the whole expanse today and was headed towards the lower end where the swamp turned into a creek to begin my search.

Blackie, Tahi, Rebel and Kuma roamed about covering ground energetically but I wasn't paying them much heed so far out from the bush. Marcus was definitely enjoying himself and asking all sorts of questions–"What were those, turkeys?"

"Yep, them's turkeys. You got them in Germany too?"

"I think so, but not in the cities."

"Yeah, gotcha."

"Gotcha? What's gotcha?"

"Gotcha? Well, you know, like 'I agree', yeah, or right on'."

"Ride on what?"

"No, no. Right on!"

"Oh," he said, more confused than ever. But I think he got the "gotcha" part all right.

Several old fences ran here and there. The wires were pretty well non-existent, or hanging in broken strands and were snarled into tangles at odd places. The place could do with some TLC.

I noticed Blackie seemed interested in something a good way ahead. He was slightly over the side of the ridge and running and stopping, running and stopping with his nose to the ground. As I watched Kuma picked up on it and started the same. He was further down the ridge, but hadn't started these antics 'til after Blackie had. I suspected something straight away and veered right, over the side. Angling down now, I came presently on some overturned earth that only a pig could have moved and pointed it out excitedly to Marcus.

"Pig-rooting Marcus. A pig has done that digging there, see? It's called pig-rooting."

"Gotcha."

"It looks like it was done last night too."

"How do you know that?"

"The dirt is still black and fresh-looking, see. That bit over there appears drier, older somehow, don't you reckon?"

"Gotcha."

"They won't be far away. Probably over the creek in that scrub there. We'll keep an eye on the dogs, especially Rebel, and be ready as soon as he barks."

Now that it seemed probable we'd get a run, I was looking forward more still to giving Marcus his first experience of pig-catching, on top of the pig hunting. Judging by the amount of talking we had been doing and the numbers of questions he'd been asking he was pretty blimin' keen. And as I saw the look of excited anticipation on his face now I was already enjoying the warm glow of giving. A pig, a pig, even a small one would do. Please?

We sauntered on, hyped-up a little I guess, eyes glued to the four dogs as they dashed about. Blackie was way down by the creek, Rebel under the big pines further ahead and Tahi and Kuma about mid-way between.

I fully expected a bark not long after the hunters entered the thick stuff across the water-course and said as much to my friend ten metres below me. He glanced around with a huge grin on his face-- anticipation. I grinned back and gave him a "thumbs up" as he pointed to Rebel, now running away at the toe of the ridge. Three hundred metres ahead, it seemed he was "onto it". Blackie was running from down where he was too, towards Rebel in the distance, and a second later Kuma took off as well. Tahi stayed fairly close for about fifteen seconds, then decided he'd better join the rest and hared away down the paddock.

Marcus and I were walking quickly now, straight down the ridge with our heads up, hands out of our pockets, breathing a little faster.

And then it happened. The westerly brought a staccato "yap-yap-yap-yap". More like Tahi's voice than Rebel's, but Rebel's it was. We broke into a pretty fast gallop as more excited barking erupted around the corner of the creek. A pig squealed then and we really hoofed it downhill. Gingerly stepping on a fallen (seemingly rotten) tree-trunk we hopped across the ditch and broke into a run again. More squealing ahead spurred us on.

The big pines towering above us in a row along the creek were fairly spaced out and had a considerable amount of older gorse growing with them. There was quite a swathe of this stuff, more or less following the course of the creek but giving way to pasture on the hillside above. From up ahead, around possibly another couple of bends in the stream the pig was squealing good-oh now. And keeping it up. Not a really small one either. The odd bark among the squealing meant they weren't all holding and I yelled to Marcus, "keep behind – me Marcus. – May be – a boar."

"Gotcha."

One last loop in the water-course loomed up, with the action just beyond. The squealing seemed pretty heavy and continuous and my knife was in my hand as I burst out of a stand of old-man gorse. Four perplexed dogs scarpered about but of the pig there was no sign, only a great big old-looking windmill. And it was going 'screek---awk, screek---awk, screek---awk as the vanes rotated around and around.

I didn't believe it! Just didn't!

It was still squealing, loudly now we were beneath it! And sounding more like a pig than you'd imagine. The dogs were still looking excited, casting around and looking about. I spent a few seconds looking dumb-founded and incredulous myself as I recall – who could blame the dogs. It was obvious to me now that Rebel, with pig-scent tantalising his mind, had heard the squeal and was off to catch an unsuspecting porker. The others were drawn in by his exuberance and all dashed along, like us, thinking they were homing in on a medium-sized pig.

I didn't quite know where to look, or what to say. But began laughing after a moment or two, joined a few seconds later by Marcus.

"Gotcha," is all he said and laughed the harder. Well, what could I say? Never in all my born days (or unborn ones for that matter) had I ever heard of such a thing. Fooled by a windmill. But as I retell the incident from time to time I leave out the "fooled by" part and recount the story of the day I caught a windmill, (and the warm glow inside went out).

Or the time Don Quixote rode again.

And Rides Again

I was pruning trees on my place one day and got a bit cheesed off when I heard a pig squealing not more than two hundred metres away. The farmer who owned the property next door wasn't too keen on pig hunters chasing the wild pigs around on his land and was known to be a dog-shooting character. How many dogs he had shot I don't really know, but I wasn't too keen on finding out with my dogs, so kept away. Now here was some cheeky poacher, right under my nose, bagging some pork that might wander one day onto my place. I thought I'd better get down there and warn the poor beggar before he got really unfortunate and had the man turn up with his gun.

My dogs were tied up at the time so all I had to do was get down off my ladder, sprint for the ute and drive away to the gate and up the road. Rather than go straight to the squeal, I decided I'd better go to my neighbour's top gate and along the track in case the poacher's vehicle was parked somewhere up that-a-way.

But no, there was no truck, and I decided the hunter, or hunters must have walked in from way over the hill.

It squealed again just then, not too far away. Between me and the creek it had to be, just through the half-grown pines. A local chap and his son were possum hunting at the time and I had given them the run of my place to help out, possum fur being the young fellow's money-spinner. And here they were right where I was heading with their 4WD bike picking up possum traps.

"Reg! Hey, where're you going mate?"

"Aw gidday Jim, Where are they?"

"Where are who? There's nobody around here, just us."

"The hunters, man. Didn't you hear the pig squeal a minute ago? Can't be too far from you fellas. You must have heard it!"

Jim looked sideways at his son on the quad, a half grin etching his face.

"Are you sure you heard a pig squeal?"

Now that made me just a wee bit ratty. After having heard 35,000 (give or take 34,000) pigs squeal, I wasn't that stupid that I didn't know what a genuine pig-squeal sounded like! He must think I'm balmy. Well, I'm not! Definitely not balmy or stupid. Stupid question more like it.

"C'mon man, I'm not that stupid. I heard a pig squeal just a minute ago, right here somewhere."

"Hey Keiran, make the pig squeal again son." Now he's like Billy T , a huge grin on his face.

"What– – ?"

Keiran revved the bike a wee bit which made it head downhill, turned a corner, then pulled hard on the handbrake.

And there it was again--squea--k! A very loud squeak actually, definitely loud enough for me to pick up over the creek and up my ladder.

I felt as stupid then as I must have looked and simply squeaked myself "Oh,"(but not very loudly.)

"We're going to fix the brakes this "arvo" Reg. Get's on your nerves a bit doesn't it!"

"I dunno, I mean yeah. A wee bit. I'd better get back--busy as. See ya."

"See ya Reg," – (still grinning).

I slunk away in an apparent (I hope) nonchalant manner in an effort to save face. (I'm not too sure it really worked though, but I never looked back.)

Blackie and Blue

Heading north from Kerikeri I was going to pick up Eddie and take him to a spot I knew of that had a hog or two left to chase. And in the dog box I had Eddie's latest up and coming learner and had been showing it the ropes recently. He was a blue heeler crossed with maybe a small beardie-type dog and reminded me so much of my Blackie of a couple of years ago. Not in size, for Eddie's dog was smallish whereas Blackie had plenty of length and a very much longer coat. Blackie was a sort of, well, black colour while Eddie's dog was a blue coloured blue-heeler called (of all things) Blue. But, if you can put aside the colour and size differences they were as alike as peas in a pod. Neither could ever keep still for more than fifteen seconds and wore out their kennel-area grass until it was dirt: or mud, depending on the weather. Blackie was tethered on a long wire and had an exercise regime that would have done an All Black proud. Up and down, up and down he'd go. First on this side, then on that side, then backwards and forwards and round and about, all day, every day. He never took holidays either and was fitter I reckon, than Ritchie McCaw.

Blue on the other hand was on a longish chain hitched to a steel spike driven in to the ground and round this at full-chain length ran this little quick-stepping budding boar stopper. I've never been able to figure out why such dogs never want to keep still. Even when my four were all lying down in the shade, or lolling in the sun, there would be Blue trotting in circles to the left, sorry right, no left again. And right again. Round and round and round and – you get the picture. I reckon Eddie's boar slayer is going to "kark-it" at not more than three years of age – worn out and run down and washed up. His over-taxed heart will just stop dead. We'll see!

But what happened to Blackie?

He never was an "A1" pig dog but nevertheless a very handy one to have when onto big boars. He was as "hard as" and accounted for the stopping of a good few porkers while in my care. I got him from Brian Armstrong as a pup because his mum was a savage, one man bitch and as mean as mean could be on Brian's cattle.

As he grew bigger and bigger and older he must have gone through a good half-dozen or more kennels of all shapes and sizes. Not content with gnawing at the kennel door surrounds he actually kept on until the whole thing was totally demolished and thus earned the sobriquet "Demolition Dog"!

But finally I was given a kennel made of half-round posts (big No one half-rounds) Full length posts made up the floor and the A-frame was more of the same though shorter. I nearly had to get a HIAB truck to bring it down to my place. In the remaining time I had Blackie he did have a good go at demolishing even that.

But one fateful day I took him north to Te Paki. Peter Greenhill and Sam Harris and I were to do another stint in the Far North scrub up that way and on a Friday we all headed off in the mid- afternoon. Sam and Peter were in Sam's Hilux and I was in my bus camper. I had to go into Kaitaia for some reason and we parted company at Awanui.

By the time I got to the camping ground at Hunter's Corner they had camp all set up but were nowhere to be found. My foray into Kaitaia had seen them arrive, do the basic setting up thing and wonder how they could while away the hours till dark and Reg's arrival.

Peter suddenly thought of a brilliant plan. "Why don't we go for a "look-see" up the hill behind camp, you know, just to get the dogs orientated and stuff?"

"Hey, that's a good idea. We might even have a pig hanging up to welcome Reg when he comes."

So away they went to chase the pork away before I even got there.

When I did "get there", I'd guessed from ten km back what they'd get up to, so simply pulled in, sited the bus on the flattest bit of ground I could find and set out to join them.

I surmised they'd go straight up the hill behind camp so decided I'd head along the road a wee way and cut up a ridge which was the left hand perimeter of a large valley covered in short scrub. My ridge turned left as I climbed and then circled back to the right, meeting the ridge I supposed Peter and Sam would be on and enclosing a valley of probably 200 acres or so.

With no real idea where my mates were, and a wind in my face I just kept climbing and watching the dogs. Rebel, who was even at that stage, my number one dog, was showing distinct signs of excitement. It would only be pigs that had him scurrying – no not scurrying. He was a very placid (normally) big dog and rather methodically poked his nose into every likely hole as if it may be the beginning of a pig-run. This was admittedly at a somewhat faster pace than usual and when I saw him with his head in the air for long seconds I knew it was only time, and he'd be away.

Tahi too was showing a lot of interest as indeed were Blackie and Kuma, any one of them likely to do the magic and put up the pig I was pretty sure was down there somewhere in the valley.

I looked away across the long south sloping hollow before me to where Peter and Sam would be but saw nothing. And on glancing ahead towards Rebel and Blackie saw nothing there either. They had gone! Ti-tree two metres tall had swallowed the pair and I only had Kuma and -, no, only Kuma. Tahi had shot into the undergrowth just as I looked. By now I was pretty hyped-up and expected developments in seconds – but they ticked by.

I stood still, anxious now that I make the right decision on where to head when they called me. I reckoned any pig with brains would head away east, climbing out of the valley if they could gain a few metres start on the finder. And that would take them directly away from me and towards Sam and Peter's section of the territory. It'd probably be better to head uphill and around if it looked like a prolonged chase and yes! – a bark from well below me. Blackie's voice this time had Kuma off into the shrubbery like lightining and heading higher than where I thought the antagonists to be! He'd know more precisely than I would just where to go and I started a tentative trot further up the ridge. Twenty metres on I stopped again. What now? Then, to my consternation, a flurry of barks and yaps from two distinctly different directions. Blackie was hard on a hog going up towards the escarpement where red claypan showed on the edge of the watershed and was probably what Kuma was homing-in on. Tahi (the yapping hound) was two hundred metres downstream in the bottom of the creek it seemed and continued his vocal challenge a few seconds after Blackie's last bark. What Rebel was up to I couldn't tell. Higher I climbed, pushing as fast as I could to the head of the valley and made it a good ten minutes after the last bark Blackie gave.

Just here, that claypan area, eroded by wind from the sea out west, was the lowest part of the valley's rim and the pigs knew it. For as I

Peter and Reg share their 110lb pig.

looked for an easy way down and across I picked out extremely fresh boar prints coming out of the fern and rubbish below me, crossing the very lowest part of the bare red ground, bearing away left towards Te Paki and Pandora, vast expanses of hakea, manuka and heavier bush. Blackie's pig!

There was no sign of dog prints though. But I guess they'd be hard to detect in the absence of any really damp ground. But I stood a while and pondered my path ahead now. To carry on around the rim towards Sam, Peter and Tahi's chase? Or turn left and along the intersecting ridge in the hope Blackie and Kuma pulled their boar?

There was a slight chance Peter and Sam's dogs may have joined Tahi, even if Rebel hadn't, and this made me opt for heading back along this far ridge above where the pigs had been camped.

With no more news from the finders I forced my way more slowly now on the slightly descending arm of the valley towards camp. I didn't realise it at the time but I would never see Blackie again and suspect now that the boar had dealt to him somewhere in that valley-head soon after his last bark. He tended to "push it" a bit and his aggressiveness may just have gotten him into trouble before back-up had arrived.

A swiftly moving shape just ahead of me stopped me dead. Then Prince, Sam's short-tailed black finder appeared in front of me, wagged

31

his stumpy appendage at me and turned back. Peter and Sam couldn't be too far away I guessed, unless Prince had been on the hunt even before Blackie had opened up. I followed along and twenty minutes later met the other two at the gate onto the grass.

"We seen it Reg. Blimin' good boar man. All black."

"Where? When? What?" I started to look around hurriedly.

"Coupla minutes ago," said Sam. "Pete and I was just watching the-fence line after the dogs barked; you know, just sort-a lookin' down there in the gut."

He was pointing to where the small creek exited the heavy scrub, a seven-wire boundary fence marking the paddock edge. The grass sloped all the way down to the road a good half-kilometre away and extended almost the same distance southwards where it met the scrub again on the far side. This meant we were in a large area of pasture surrounded by manuka fern and flaxes, cabbage and coprosma trees, hakea and gorse and many other species that made up this northern backblocks pig habitat.

Peter joined in now. "How Rebel missed it I don't know. It just bolted straight across the grass and disappeared into the far side by that big cabbage tree at the corner. See?" He pointed to an angle in the boundary fence about half-way down. "Rebel appeared on his track as he topped the rise there (half-way across) and loped along good-oh! We thought for sure he was on the scent, but he seems to have missed it."

Just then he opened up. Some vicious barking, quite unlike him really, a loud squeal, and we were off. Bolting downhill across the corner of the paddock, we raced for the action. I could still race pretty good then and beat Sam and Peter, leaping over the wires with a hand on a post.

Rebel had been joined by one of Sam's dogs and a fine squeal guided us in. No boar this time though. Only a 70lber, a sow even, was hastily taken off the dogs and chased away (didn't have to do much chasing).

That boar must have been very lucky to have found another pig to confuse it's pursuers like it had. And no doubt it was still trotting away deeper into the cover behind us.

"A pig's a pig" Rebel thought more than likely, and settled for an easy one. The boar would keep!

A Very Good, Very Keen Man

Eddie is the original good keen man. Indeed he goes even one better than Barry Crump's hero, in that he is a very good, very keen man. Almost to the extent of being nearly as keen as myself. Now we are not talking about stamp collecting, or even crocheting, super-exciting as they may be. No, no! He is in actual fact, yes, you guessed it, a tried and true pig hunter. The tried part refers to his having tried it a number of times with varied success and now is truly hooked.

"Your dogs any good at present Reg?" he asked.

Well! How to answer? If I said yes, he'd possibly think I was bragging and also leave myself open to future ridicule. And if I said no, I'd maybe miss out on some forthcoming invitation to hunt a "big'un." So I came up with "uh-huh," sort of" (fairly safe and fairly true)

"Good boar stoppers?"

"Uh-huh, sort of."

"You keen for a run on Saturday then?"

"Uh-huh."

"Your missus won't mind if you come?"

"Sort of.""Ahhh."

A couple of minutes went by in silence, then with a side long glance, "I know where there's a good one we'd probably get onto, I'll bring Snow and Whatiwhati. Between us we ought to clobber him." (We eventually left Snow at home)

"Let's see," I thought. "This is Monday isn't it? If I tidy up the shed tonight, do the GST Tuesday night, fix the tail lights on Olive's car Wednesday night, finish wallpapering the spare bedroom on Thursday night, that'll leave Friday night to mow the lawns by torchlight. With a little bit of luck I'll have a half hour before midnight to get my gear ready and put the dog-box on the ute. So you'd better tell me about it."

A huge grin broke out when he realised it was most likely all on.

"It's on a place I've hunted at a time or two in the past and certainly isn't afraid of dogs at all."

"How do you know?" I asked

"He actually waits for the dogs and then rips into them like nothing you've ever seen man. Tosses his head around and chases them round and round in the ti-tree and gorse and then bolts for the thickest stand of mangi-mangi he can find and waits again."

"You ever seen him?" – cautiously

"Nope, never have. But Richard has. Some mate of his took two packs of dogs one day and put him up almost straight away. He was in that confounded mangi-mangi again and dealt to three dogs what never made it. The others wouldn't go in again after that so he's still there somewhere."

"Anyone else ever chase him?"

"Yup! He's killed a few other dogs apparently – some blokes from down south somewhere. But they were all holders and I reckon your dogs'll be able to bail him easy enough without getting into too much trouble. What do you reckon?"

I was reckoning it didn't sound too good. I mean, my too main dogs knew what to do, but the two others were really only learners of two years. And never having been up against a real fighter, well, anything might happen. In their exuberance and youthful inexperience, they'd more than likely mistake his lying in wait for bewilderment and fear and get too close before they figured it all out. Then I'd only have two dogs left to start again. And no, I didn't like the sound of it. But yes, I would like to try none-the-less – I think.

"Is he always in the same place Eddie? Roughly?"

"Not always. Sometimes he's nowhere to be seen at all, in fact, no one's seen him for about six months now, maybe he's died. Or moved on – or something."

Eddie's enthusiasm for putting my team in front of this dog-eater was being watered down by my obvious reticence. Yet he'd picked up that I'd like to have a look around the property concerned all the same.

"Tell you what. What say I have a look during the week, and if I don't see his big marks anywhere after work it'd probably be safe to go for a walk eh!"

"Yeah, that'd be a good idea Eddie. I'll ring you Thursday evening before I start the wallpapering and you can let me know how safe it is.

Hang on, perhaps I'd better finish the wallpapering first eh!"

Now while I love wallpapering, I love the end of it even more and was thankful at last to pack all the gear away and give Eddie a phone call. He answered on the first ring and was, if anything it seemed, keener still to have a look around.

"There's still no sign of that big fella Reg. Can't work out where he's gone. But there's still a pig or two around going by the rooting I've seen."

"Good size rooting?"

"Eh?"

"I mean how deep is this rooting you're talking about? You can tell fairly well by the size of the holes they are making. May even see a heavy footprint if you look hard enough. A little pig can't plough up as much as a big boar obviously. So what do you reckon?"

He was thinking of course as I was talking and came back with an estimation of at least one good pig of around 100lbs at least. He hadn't noticed any clear marks but that rooting was definitely more than what a weaner could do.

We had arranged to meet at the farm gate an hour before day-break and as we said "good morning" it became apparent that it might not actually be quite so. On the drive from my place there had been an occasional drop of moisture on the windscreen. But now this gave way to something a bit more like heavy drizzle and made me put my butterfly cape on and grab a peaked hat. (Hoods are okay but I prefer to have a peak keeping the front of the cape/hood above my eyes a bit more)

Eddie was raring to go and we set off through a stand of pine trees heading for some scattered gorse and grass (and mangi-mangi) two gullies over. He had along a youngish heading type dog while I too had an extra. Grandson Sean Laybourn and I couldn't decide who actually owned Tubby, a big red mastiff/lab cross dog who took great delight of tormenting the ears of wild pigs if given the chance. Some weeks he was with Sean in Whangarei (who really did own him) and the other weeks he ran with the pack and thought I owned him – or he owned me. A really lovely natured dog he is, and worth his considerable weight in gold on big boars when Rebel (encouraged I'm sure by the presence of Tubby) decided he was a holder instead of a bailer.

And with the vague possibility of coming across "Mr Big" I unconsciously reverted to "holder" mentality again and was quietly relieved he was along.

The pace Eddie set as he headed off was one I hoped he wouldn't keep up for long. Maybe it was just to get warm amidst the constant raindrops. His bush shirt would get heavy soon and slow him down just a mite – and I just might be able to keep him in sight.

The first gully, still within the pines had a raupo-infested pond where we crossed and here in the muddy edges near the water we saw boar marks. Big boar marks! Really big boar marks in fact!

Omigosh!

On looking intensely it was figured they weren't last night's though and I looked again at Tubby and Rebel and wondered how they'd fare if we raised him later in the day, or on a subsequent visit. Still not sure about the wisdom of having him along I was thinking it would be better to target "Mr Big" with maybe Rebel and Tahi by themselves. Rebel really was a pretty good back-end stopper and Tahi too did the business really well and I found myself leaning towards the idea of using just those two experienced pooches when I learned more of his whereabouts.

Cogitating thus I lifted my eyes to find Eddie had disappeared and was all set to head higher and crack on the pace when I heard the fence "ping" somewhere below me. He'd taken the dogs with him too, except for Tubby, so I crept downhill a way to where a pig track traversed the second gully and headed to the same fence.

There were no new marks on the road though and a minute later I was standing with Eddie at the pop-hole under the wire.

"Dogs have gone Reg," breathed Eddie.

"Where?"

He pointed out into the mangi-mangi and gorse his side of the fence and waved his arm left and downslope.

"Seemed pretty keen the whole four of them. My fella went too" He was all serious in anticipation and kept his head cocked as he listened intently above the breeze.

Tubby worked his way towards the swamp on our left and was soon out of sight too and we stopped a while longer. All was quiet as dawn hovered over the far hill, inching slowly but perceptibly nearer. The rustles and scrapings of the undergrowth seemed to intensify marginally now with the awakening of the day, the wind stiffening somewhat from out towards the lightening sky. Ti-tree bent and moved and bent again to each huff and puff and I strained to decipher the umpteen small sounds borne our way.

But the bark never came. The reappearance of Bud and Shiney, followed almost immediately by Eddie's dog induced us to leave the fence and move on slowly down the shallow depression we were in. Eddie was in front and moved ahead steadily, ducking and weaving among the manuka and gorse. I was pleased to follow at the moment; he could glean most of the raindrops hanging on the foliage and so leave a drier path for me to traverse in his wake. Cobwebs were common too and I noticed him swiping at his face from time to time as he forged ahead.

Coming to where another shallow gully intersected from our right, he glanced around.

"I reckon we'll head up here on to the ridge eh Reg? It's not too far and we'll be able to hear better from higher up."

I nodded, hands in pockets and stepped off again to traipse along. Where he had altered course was marshy, soft and wet underfoot and I noticed the first faint awareness of dampness seeping through my rugby boots. He was in short "Red-bands" and apparently wasn't too concerned where the path led, pugged-up cow tracks, water filled hollows and squelchy mud all the same to him. I worked more assiduously at keeping my feet drier than would otherwise be the case and lapsed behind a wee bit.

He was waiting on the rise though and still staring out across the valley and I pulled up alongside. Away over were small black dots on the grass among the gorse patches, too big to be pigs – I think. I was watching them intently in the growing light hoping I'd be proved wrong when the shadows faded.

Still those three dogs away! There must be something about to be holding their attention for so long and I allowed myself to hope a little bit more.

But just then Rebel arrived, clean as a whistle, from uphill towards the pinetrees and a few seconds later Tahi appeared from the same direction and my hopes subsided again.

Tubby, quite capable of finding a pig on his own wasn't, or hadn't yet proved to be great shakes at the business of stopping the pigs so we moved on slowly, downhill once more into what appeared to be more mangi-mangi and gorse.

The wind had dropped if anything and the sky was iron grey, hard and sombre and seemed somehow menacing and aloof. Rain still spattered at it's whim and we had to keep moving to keep warm. And in this vein we pushed along beneath the taller manuka at the runnel edge. Not yet a stream, the water in the gutter gurgled along at quite a rate with the addition of the precipitation of the last several hours.

Pig marks were evident at various places though nothing big had been about of late. Rebel got interested though when we came to an old silted-up damn and saw boar marks made not twenty-four hours ago. They headed in the general direction that we were going, into taller manuka where he once more moved out of sight. Light was still vague beneath the canopy of the trees and it was pretty well nigh impossible to be searching successfully for hoof prints in the ground ahead of us here.

An hour went by without anything exciting happening and we ended up at the far end of the shallow catchment area that spawned the small water-course we had travelled along.

"What now Eddie?" I asked.

"Dunno. There's definitely pigs around – somewhere. Maybe we could head back that-a-way," he returned, pointing in the direction of where we had come, though this time to the right more and down a long leading ridge.

There was a small open area of grass along the ridge top that was slowly losing the battle to the encroaching gorse. This was where he was hoping we'd get lucky. He could well be correct, for as we got underway it was apparent that the swine we were looking for had been frequenting the area more so than where we were previously. Hoof marks and rooting were evident to quite some degree and I felt quite keyed up. Tubby had turned up prior to our new direction-sally and for a time seemed happy to stay with me.

"Hey, look at this Reg, come over here man." Eddie was pointing at the ground where the cattle had killed the gorse and left a muddy trail. "That's pretty fresh isn't it? What do you reckon?"

"Hah! Big billy-goat, can't you tell?"

He looked at me quizzically and then pointed emphatically at the marks again. "What's them then? Big billy-goat my great aunt Agatha!"

"Them then" were dew-claw marks to the rear of what looked like a 150lb boar's finger-prints.

"Your great aunt Agatha would turn over in her grave Ed," I came back with. I had noted we only had his dog left with us and my attitude of listening while I was talking pretty well gave the lie to my bluffing.

"Them marks are obviously where the goat put his hind feet in the same place as his front ones – double marks, see!"

"I know I look dumb, but in actual fact I'm not. Them there's boar marks and you know nothing about it obviously, but hang around, you'll learn – maybe."

He wasn't grinning, but there was a little smirk he was trying to hide and kept his face averted.

"Yeah! Yeah! Yeah!" I said. "Let's push on eh?"

The rain was actually rain now. Not drizzle anymore but not yet heavy either and it was good to be in action again to keep warm. Dogs came and went and after half an hour we'd pretty well covered the ground we'd set out to do and were looking to head on back.

I had a strange feeling though, one I can't describe and suggested nonchalantly that we could have one last try at a ridge heading back and up to our right, towards more open farmland yet. That vague something was growing and pulling me upslope even as I suggested it and Eddie fell in behind for once.

"You're determined to find your billy-goat aren't you?" he offered.

"Yep! We'll go just a wee way and then cut back down that small opening in the gorse. Won't take us more'n twenty minutes – you never know."

My plan didn't have much more to offer as we'd gone threequarters of the distance and were now in that small opening in the gorse. A dry water course was over-grown by biggish gorse and I picked my way through to emerge in a small open space of kikuyu.

With all the pooches present, the sudden eruption of running, bounding dogs took us by some surprise. Back they all six went into heavy gorse and disappeared with no noise. Eddie and I stopped dead and held our breath.

Fifteen seconds is a long time just so, and when the barking started below us we hastily replenished the air in our lungs and hit the scrub at a run. Noises came and went and came again but were moving away into bigger cover. We careered in the wake of the chase but kept slightly lower because of the more open ground along the creek. No thought was given now to keeping feet or clothing dry in the wet undergrowth and we pounded along, dodging and weaving and stopping hurriedly to listen.

"Up this gutter Reg," Eddie had left me and veered right into heavier gorse. I turned and followed straight away. Here the ground rose and as we neared the sounds that told of a caught pig I handed Eddie the knife as he was in front.

He stopped real quick. "No! No! You do it Reg. I'll stuff it up."

Eddie, Whatithati and the 144 pounder hanging from a tree.

"No you won't, have a go."

But he was thrusting the knife at me as he stepped hastily aside and we swapped. Taking the knife I nonetheless off-loaded my rifle to him as I went past. With the battle in full swing just over a small rise I could tell there would be no chance or need to use the gun. The boar's grunting mingled with the crashing and puffing and wheezing of five dogs told me all too plainly of the desperation in the air. And I could FEEL it.

The broken-coloured boar tried to lunge ahead and go right but Tubby was in the way and hampering it's progress. With Rebel on the other ear the pig had not much chance other than to pull ahead and even this inclination soon left him as Tahi bit him repeatedly on his nuts. The scraunching of wire and the difficulty I was having in getting between Rebel and the boar's ribcage finally told me there was a fence, right here. I was leaning over it, unaware it was there, trying to get all

In the steady rain Eddie hefted the animal and turned back into the bigger manuka.

the fern and gorse away so I could stick the animal. I ended up leaping over, almost upending over the pig's snout and stumbling beyond before righting myself and coming back to do the business on Tubby's side.

Poor old Mr Pig. Isn't it strange, the feeling of regret now he's dead. One of awe, respect and even chagrin that our foe is no more and has lost his last battle. A certain amount of disappointment for the pig, tempers somewhat the elation and euphoria the winning of the chase and battle generally engenders and I could almost imagine to myself another fellow boar swapping yarns of other hunts and escapades with our now dead warrior.

What revelry there would be as they grunted and squealed and huffed and stepped about, swinging their heads left and right, up and down, feinting and thrusting in the retelling of some of their more memorable foilings of the dogs.

"Yeah that black one with the stumpy tail's a mean 'un! He's been on me five times that I can recall – hard to throw off my track the brute, nearly got me last month. Must be getting old eh Bart?"

"I know the brute too well myself cuzzy. I found if I stood my ground and chased him vigorously before the others turned up he'd not try too hard. The coward will wait for his mates just enough I find to let me slip away after that."

"Yep, yep they don't seem to like the rough ---"

But no, I'm not the boar, and Eddie's rambling on enthusiastically and grinning hugely in spite of the steady rain now and, what was that he asks?

"I'm not too sure Ed. Where is he?"

He had inquired re Rebel's wounded back leg and I was searching the vicinity for my number one dog so I could look myself.

"Here Rebel! Here Rebel!"

He came limping to me looking all wet and bedraggled and covered in gorse prickles, and with a nasty four inch gash on his hip. But it wasn't really serious. Even the two small nicks on Tubby weren't anything to worry about either and Buddy's poke in his chest was hardly noticeable. Tahi, Shiney and Eddie's dog were unmarked and we thankfully set about gutting the pig beside the overgrown fence.

In the steady rain Eddie hefted the animal and turned back into the bigger manuka, heading for home and some dry clothes.

I was fairly wet too and beginning to feel uncomfortable at the cessation of really strenuous activity. We pushed ahead valiantly but got boxed in by heavier and heavier gorse until at last we dumped the pig and searched for a way through. We nearly lost it as it happened. Trying to find him again in all that confounded Scottish prickle nearly had us beat. But as last, wet through and colder now, we stumbled upon it, decided to leave it hanging from a tree at the edge of the grass and hoofed it for the truck a mile away. Took some photos too before we set sail.

"Remarkable how much he resembles a big billy-goat like that eh Reg?" This time I definitely saw him grin and grinned back myself.

"Right on man. Like a 143lb billy-goat don't you reckon?" And away we went to come back later with a quad for the pork. We were actually one pound too light in our guess of his weight.

Up A Side Gully

It was a blustery, squally day a few years ago when I went walkabout up Goshen way. It'd been a while since I was here and I noticed the encroaching vegetation on the track. Small gorse plants were now little shrubs and manuka sprouted out of the clay where before there was just roadway and hoofmarks. Even kumarahoe was more profuse at this time of year (early spring) and was now a golden yellow among the green.

I was heading for "the graves" a small way ahead yet and up a small steep climb. Well, the vicinity of the graves to be more correct. It was about here some years ago that I came face to face with a large black boar and I was wondering if he still presided over the general area. Certainly I hadn't caught him for he was very distinctive. A small off-white patch on his right shoulder and another on his right front leg would've been readily identifiable had he gone down to my pack of dogs. Neither had I heard of a pig bearing his description being taken from hereabouts by anyone else.

The day I met him I had turned left off the track and headed generally uphill beneath the pines and among the underbrush aiming for another track 300 to 400 metres distant.

All my dogs were at heel, indeed had been since leaving the grass twenty minutes ago and I bent my head to duck beneath a branch at about shoulder level. As I looked up again I saw this large boar standing stock still only six metres in front of me and before a large macrocarpa tree. And in a half split-second he was gone, bolting away and downhill to the right. Yep! The dogs did see him and gave chase enthusiastically – you betcha. His slight lead became slightly less slight and fairly soon fairly considerable, until eventually the returning dogs told me it had become very huge. It's one of those "should have been, but wasn't" episodes we've all had I guess and I was hugely disappointed. But I would try another day again I reckoned – today!

While not branching off to where I'd seen him that day, I was confident I would put him up was he handy, so carried slowly on towards the cemetery.

Tahi and Rebel were keen, and doing their thing regularly and conscientiously. Scouting about and checking the runways, I could sense they were just as eager to chance upon a whiff of the hog of not so long ago, as I was to see a fresh print or few.

I bypassed a track up to the graves and turned right instead. Just below a little way, a stream dribbled hurriedly and gurgled between the fallen logs that once spanned as a bridge but now lay strewn all higgledy-piggledy every which way. Flash floods and heavy rain often enough swelled the flow of runoff, undermined the abutments (if you could have called them that) and collapsed the banks, until now only one log remained as a crossing.

I stepped down gingerly, balancing as best I could and hopped eventually onto the clay bank a metre below the original ground level. Fortunately a small ti-tree still grew atop the rise and I pulled myself up onto the grassy flat. Grassy? Used to be! Now it was gorsey more like. Seems it got less grass and more gorse each winter, so that now it was a real nightmare finding the track on the other side. No trouble for Tahi and Rebel though. The prick eared brindle staffy-cross and light brown quarter-whippet were well below the dangerous stiff green spikes anyway and had disappeared again going in the same direction as I intended.

Being low down in the valley I couldn't see much beyond the immediate hills but guessed black clouds were somewhere beyond the skyline because of the almost continuous low rumble of thunder. The air was suddenly cooler and I knew rain wasn't far off.

Shiney and Bud stayed at heel all the way to the top of the climb. Here a fence crossed over and as I negotiated that the two learners shot off around the side of the spur. Their gait told of urgency of interest beyond the head-high gorse and I ploughed through in a hurry.

An open patch of grass saw me stop and hold my breath. No noise yet. Wind – yes! But barking – no. Rebel and Tahi were probably somewhere in the valley before me and I was hopeful of a bark momentarily. But none came. I looked at my watch and again fifteen minutes later, and at the expanse of scrub below and in front of me. In these moments I was planning where to run when the barking came. Which vaguely remembered trail I should follow or pig track to flounder along? Maybe, if they barked yonder, it'd be better to go the long way around on the

Reg with Bud, and the boar.

more even ground. The vehicle track was yet fairly open and so offered an easier route along the head of the valley. That way too, I could revise my plan should the chase veer one way or another.

A dog barked behind me and a few seconds later again. The next bark a few seconds later still came from maybe 100 metres to the left but across the stream in the gully. Here a grove of ponga clad the eastern slope below the young pines, right down to the water, and just now hid from view a pretty large wild boar. His enraged snort, a dog's yip, and then a more savage stint of barking told of a confrontation a quarter-kilometre below where I was.

I was halfway there, expecting to either hear the two pups arrive, or see them bolt past, when all went quiet. I stopped immediately to listen more intently. Nothing came to alleviate my fears of a complete getaway. And as the minutes ticked away the boar got bigger and bigger. I mean, a 100lb pig was not likely to escape those two experienced hog-hounds, had to be pushing 120lb maybe.

A very short flurry of barking came for a few seconds up near the damn just then, "he's climbing" I conceded wondering. Had to be 140lb now surely. And exceedingly fit and fast to go uphill and pull ahead as he had. Rebel and Tahi both were no slouches in the tight stuff themselves, and here he had drawn away, only to be hauled in again possibly at the dam itself with it's more open area adjoining. But again he was able to leap away. A feint at Rebel and a lunge at Tahi saw them hastily back off just enough to convince him it was safe to turn and run again.

Bud had come back to me about now and had only just shot into the scrub immediately at the short bail when it evaporated again.

"Darn!" Nothing for it but to head back to the track once more. This time Shiney was waiting at the fence, having come straight up from the dam. Probably she had been close when the older two had forced the pig to bail, but had just missed out and been left wondering which way to go after she had burst out onto where they had been.

Now us three stood on an open patch of grass and waited. There was no use in charging off anywhere as I had no idea in what direction to charge.

Shiney and Bud had moved off a small distance and I was looking in the opposite direction to the dam. This was where the "bone arrow boar" used to hold sway and I go to wondering where he was now-a-days. The curve of the stream brought a ridge or spur down from the log landing, covered in bush and fairly steep. A good way off it was and had I not been looking directly that way, may well have missed the small insignificant sound wafted down the valley.

But that sound, insignificant and small to anyone else maybe, was hugely telling to a tensed-up keenly listening pig hunter! Something was going on up there. The twenty minutes since the bail at the dam was just about enough to allow a wild pig on the run, time to cover even that considerable distance. In an intense effort to hear I was moving my head right and left, mouth open, holding my breath. And I heard it again. A sound indefinable, yet different. And just different enough to launch me at the gorse in front of me. A short distance was covered before I burst out onto slightly more open terrain where a fence ran down the hill. Here I stopped again and stared off towards the head of the valley. No noise came this time that I could hear, and I had just started to doubt what I thought I had previously listened to, when Shiney and Bud both took off straight for where I was headed. They must have heard something I couldn't. Off I went again. Downhill a hundred metres and into tallish manuka and pine trees. Being down in the heavier bush soon after, I was out of audio range I knew, but pressed on, gradually getting lower as I headed for the creek at it's confluence with another slightly larger stream.

Ten minutes saw me at the water and as I crossed at a pig-run I was hoping I was heading off up the right ridge. Several small gutters with intersecting spurs converged more or less where the creeks met and I could only keep my fingers crossed as I began to climb hurriedly for the top.

Nearly half way there I heard the sounds that spurred me on. The "yip" and crash, sticks snapping, heavy breathing, a snort. All battle sounds, now clearly audible, had me pushing it yet again. On a small flat, twenty metres off and above me I saw the white of Shiney moving about, accompanied by black and fawn shapes, and shades of shadows.

The rain and I arrived at the same time, but the boar, only about 110lb took no notice of either event. He had quite good hooks on him but seemed incapable of using them to any good effect. He just staggered about as Tahi, Rebel and Shiney pulled on his ears and Bud hung onto his hock.

It was easy enough now to despatch him and sit on his ribcage gasping lung fulls of air. How good it felt to be successful again, to have finally run down a good pig in it's own domain. To have had my two main dogs persevere a considerable distance and succeed in the end.

I patted them all, and came away with blood on my hand from Bud. The boar had after all used his tusks and inflicted a nasty-looking wound on his flank. But it was only skin, not flesh that was torn, and I heaved a sigh of relief. Tahi too had a small poke on his snowy chest, but wasn't fazed by it.

Yippee! Yahoo! We'd done it again.

The hard work of gutting it and carrying it was made worse by the rain. Constant and heavy now, it had me wet through and uncomfortable in no time. The small climb up and across the ridge to the track I knew was there, convinced me to shuck my burden and return later with Mark's 4x4 bike. Much, much easier! It was almost the identical place to where Peter Greenhill and I had caught a 140lber some years goneby, and to where I had left another boar caught by Fred the dog, also long ago.

And some months later still, the same four dogs caught an identical

To have finally run down a good pig.

pig, a boar of 107lb. in heavier gorse on the next ridge over. A brother – litter-mate? More than likely.

Hanging In There

"Reg? Eddie."

"Oh, hi Eddie. I guess you're not ringing to inquire after my health."

"No, absolutely not. Actually I was wondering how you're placed for Saturday."

He doesn't beat around the bush much, gets straight to the "nitty-gritty" does Eddie.

"To be absolutely truthful I was going to go hunting. I know you find that hard to believe, but it's true. Was going to ring you actually, what's up?"

"Jamie's heard of a good pig out the back. Some of his mates chased it last weekend but it blew their dogs away. I thought you might be interested. Unfortunately though . . ."

"What?" (Surely it hadn't been caught mid-week.)

"Seems I can't make it mate – work – you know."

"Aw gee Eddie, I was hoping you could tag along. That's disappointing man. Where's this pig?"

"You know the damn off Jodie's Road where we split up last time. Somewhere in that area. You'll know it if you see it. It's gingery white and big. They were just letting their dogs out and hadn't even got the gun out of the ute when this dirty great boar charged out of the gorse in the paddock and came straight at them. Lucky for them one of their dogs got in the way and it ran off opposite that dam."

"And they didn't' get it?"

"It killed their main dog and they pretty-well chucked it in after that," he replied. "I'll lend you my cellphone so you can call me if you get lucky. If you come about seven o'clock you can go in the usual way and park in the pines."

"Yeah. Righto Eddie, see you then." I was already excited about running into Mr Boar. The chances were good I reckoned. Having got away scot free and not being chased, probably made him think he was safe-as. Was this the same big dog-killer Richard had spoken of some time ago? More than one dog had been dealt to by this huge grandfather of a pig. Several chaps from Auckland had tried to nail him with two teams of dogs – but got towelled-up horrendously. Apparently he'd run for the densest patch of mingi-mingi when the dogs put him up, and bail in there where you've got no show of using a gun and the dogs can't manoeuvre adequately. I dreaded the stuff and hoped against hope that should I find him he'd head for the gorse instead.

It was with exhilaration mixed with trepidation that I fronted up to Eddies' at 6.45am next morning. I guess it's one of those cases of "It'll not happen to me."

In my imagination I'd work for three hours and finally put him up almost back at the truck. Rebel, or Tahi would winkle him out of his lair high up on the edge of that slip where the cutty-grass grew, and down he'd come to bail momentarily while gathering his wits. Only he'd now know that I was standing there behind a hakea bush with my rifle pointing (my loaded rifle pointing) to where he was standing. I'd pull the trigger and be an instant celebrity among the hunting fraternity who know of him and his fearsome reputation.

With Eddie's phone in my jacket pocket now I had already passed the cutty-grass slip and heaved a sigh of relief. No pig. Hey – this is crazy. I'm supposed to be looking for a pig – a boar in fact and here I was feeling lucky I hadn't been lucky. Must be losing my touch.

On such a lovely day pig hunting really comes into it's own. Whether or not I catch a pig is of lesser importance to the enjoyment of the wilderness. The blue of the sky and the clouds winging by take my mind far away. The hills far off of green and darker green beckon me on – I'd love to walk them all, but doubt I'll get there today. Still, who knows, I'm probably the only human being for miles and miles and all this is my domain. Doesn't the mind conjure up some weird and far-out ideas?

As I dropped lower and lower towards the creek the sunlight came less effectively through the canopy and shadows darkened into gloom a small way off. The sighing of the wind through the pines was a decidedly lullaby sound, soothing and peaceful and even the dogs seemed half asleep.

I was angling down steeper now aiming to go around several ridges and arrive at the pond Eddie spoke of, from the bottom side. The pines were bigger here too, maybe an earlier planting and appeared ready to harvest. And as a result, the under-storey was more open and easier to get through without making a lot of noise. Generally I don't worry over much about keeping very quiet. If the pig is close enough to hear the crackling of underbrush, he's close enough for a half-pie finder to suss him out I reckon! My finders were half-pie to three-quarter-pie today, and I pushed on in the shade with my head bent, looking at my footing. No good would come of me twisting my ankle away out here by myself (Ah, the phone!) My ankles do tend to be weak actually (along with my head according to some) and when a youngster, was recommended to wear boots rather than shoes, as extra ankle support. But my rugby boots don't let me slide around too much and I rarely hunt without them – and intend to get some high-profile ones come summer out of deference to those weak ankles.

Quite out of the blue I plummeted-cum-slid, holding onto little bushes, onto a good sized forest road metalled by pine needles. I turned left here and strolled along for about twenty minutes. Then on rounding a corner, the silence was broken by the sound of frogs entering the water.

Plop, plop splash! And there, straight ahead on the left of the road, was the pond. Thick green reeds stood a metre tall out of the water and small floating light-green weed, flattish and pale, sat at the edges.

Dark green and deep, the water seemed sombre and brooding. What chilling secrets hid beneath the surface ready to be borne aloft on the wings of the dragonflies that darted and hovered incessantly. There were dozens of the big black insect-helicopters about, careering and backing up and zooming off again. But they didn't seem to be going anywhere. We were though. I angled off through the trees on the right heading more directly for a gully I knew of which had some good patches of fern in it. Pig sign had been plentifully evident there on a previous visit and I thought it may be productive to look again. Meanwhile the almost complete absence of hoof-marks on the ground was a disappointment. Even if you don't come across any rooting, you'd generally see pig tracks on runways and trails that get made as they move about. So judging by what I saw today, or didn't see, there were no pigs for miles around.

Rebel had stayed pretty well at heel ever since leaving the frog pond and while I was enjoying the walk knew I would be even more so if he were out scouting around. He's not the world's best finder and most often only goes when there is a scent. Once it was found though, Rebel seemed somehow more capable of running the scent out to it's maker. Obviously there was no pig in this patch of the woods.

"Woof! Woof! Woof!" Over behind me. Only Bud was away and in the same direction.

Within seconds a "Woof! Woof! Woof!" again, and a big black shape was seen flitting through the trees on my left, "going like the clappers" and heading for my gully. All the dogs were now in strenuous action, Bud in the lead a short way and striving hard. The boar was going pretty good though and kept his lead – just. As he disappeared over the rim of the gully I could see Rebel had caught up to Bud and they chased their quarry out of sight, followed immediately by Tahi. There had been absolutely no opportunity for a shot with the rifle – too many tree trunks.

Goodbye pig? The hour-long half-minute finally gave way to savage barking. They seemed to have stopped him in a plantation of pampas halfway down the side where a small flat protruded.

A vigorous shaking of the cutty-grass was followed just then by snorting and stomping noises. This was one very annoyed pig and getting rather worked up. More crashing about and out shot Tahi and Bud, heading for the hills. They stopped though when they realised they were still in one piece (make that two) and turned and began barking vociferously. I couldn't see what exactly they were barking at, but knew it was one considerable-sized baconer.

But where was Rebel? I snuck around the far side of the pampas and saw an opening just large enough for – what? While manoeuvering around the cutty-grass I was very conscious of Tahi and Bud, seen out of the corner of my eye. They were really going "berko" at something in there. But having none of it. Well out of the way they were, barking encouragement and defiance, probably in that order! Encouragement to Rebel hanging in there, by himself, doing the work in the danger zone. What I was looking at in fact.

There was this defiant, thoroughly aroused and cantankerous wild boar, jet black and huge-looking with an equally aroused and very determined fawn dog clamped onto his left ear.

Backwards and forwards they went. Then round and round. Then sideways and ahead, and back again. Rebel didn't seem to be able by himself to hamper the pig's movement over much but was doing his part as best he could.

Bud and Tahi were faithfully backing him up, audibly, from a safe ten metres uphill. Very admirable that, lending moral support when at any moment they could be charged – or even ripped and hurt badly.

Eddie Broderick with Rebel's 116lb once cantankerous boar.

How commendable! They were relying on Rebel to do the deed. They reckoned he was pretty good!

Well, me too. But I guessed he was cussing under his breath, (if he had any to spare) and berating his two mates for leaving him to it.

You can imagine his thoughts – "It's all very well for you two to yabber your heads off out there. Get in here and give me a hand! Now!"

It was apparent that for reasons of their own, they weren't going to though, and I realised that I had to do something myself to help Rebel out.

Raising my .44 I sighted-in on Mr. Bristle-back's front shoulder and squeezed off a shot . At only eight or nine metres that should have been the end. It was – of the "status-quo." Things certainly changed rapidly. Mr. Boar was galvanised into instant action and charged ahead, disappearing from that tunnel in the foliage before me. But next instant he was back, but turned around, for there was faithful old Rebel, still hanging in there on his left ear. Now I could see him better and put another bullet at the boar's hindquarters. That too went in with a solid "whumph". But to no apparent effect, other than ensuring they spun around again.

I could see Rebel was tiring and felt desperate as to what more I could do. Red on his frontquarters wasn't a good sign and I fretted as I raised the gun one last time.

This time I put the ammo right in the middle of the pig's guts. And boy, did I get results! He disappeared.

Bud and Tahi had stopped their barking now and were camped around to my right and certainly no closer. The only thing they were doing was peering pointedly at some more cutty-grass twenty metres away.

I had seen the fern and small ground cover shake and wave about as the two battlers departed my pampas bush. Heading away almost opposite to where I was, they were out of sight almost immediately, and all I became aware of after exiting my position was total silence and lack of movement. No pig, no Rebel, only the two guard-dogs pointing further ahead.

But I knew! The noise that last bullet made on impact told me it was all over, or would be very presently. Gingerly I parted the rubbish in front of me and began to work my way ever so cautiously forwards. Was he dead yet? Or waiting for me just ahead?

But with no movement or noise, and Rebel slowly coming my way from ten metres below at an angle, I was almost certain the boar was down and done for.

I searched for perhaps ten minutes and couldn't find him; he must be here somewhere! I parted the fronds of the pampas Bud and Tahi were so interested in and came face to face with our foe. A metre away now and almost at face level to me as I stopped, he nevertheless gave me a start. But all belligerence was gone. He lay on his right side seemingly intact, but vanquished now. And ascertaining that he was truly dead, I turned to look at Rebel.

"Rebel, here Rebel old mate. Let's see how you fared, you marvellous old warrior."

He came slowly, and wagged his tail as I felt along his back and sides. And patted him, making a real fuss to let him know how pleased I was with his solo performance. Sitting down, I put an arm around him and talked quietly while his two canine acquaintances crept closer. Not interested in their share of patting and congratulations, they inched their way forwards to inspect the pig. Bud was growling continuously, low in his throat and still didn't get too close. Tahi was bolder and checked the boar out at close quarters and then came to me reckoning he was due for some praise too. But didn't get more than a pat. I couldn't bring myself to castigate him really – or BuddyBuddy. Why they had chucked the towel in so uncharacteristically was beyond me.

In talking to various other hunters I've been told yarns of their dogs doing very much the same. For some peculiar reason or other, a certain boar will mysteriously "spook" a dog, or dogs, which results in them having nothing to do with it. To the extent that returning to the pig's territory on subsequent visits gets the same response. They'll find the pig and come straight off it time and again. Some other boar, and bang! they've got him. Or another hunter's dog will not be at all phased by his aura, or mana, or whatever it is, and nail him on the spot.

Tahi and Bud have found and caught boars before and since, no problem, but this one? No way!

They must have seen something Rebel hadn't and got the wind-up properly. Still, it was a good run and a good accounting by Rebel in stopping our 116lber.

And medals? Both Bud and Rebel had a couple of superfluous pokes, or rips really and I guess we were lucky considering the boar's excellent set of hooks. I'm prepared to let Tahi and Bud hang in there yet too; I suppose anyone can have an off day now and again.

If You Can't Beat 'Em Sit Down

A lot that goes into making a young pig dog a successful one comes from the way it is trained early on. Not too many rise through the ranks as "also-rans" and then develop into ace finder/stoppers later in life. There is of course the situation where a promising dog comes into it's own on the retirement of the number one animal in the pack, when it finds it is not out-gunned and out-found by the "Boss dog" and realises it is up to it to do that part of the job now.

My Flash of some years ago was constantly out-found by Bing until the day I heard the chase coming towards me, promising to cut over the track some fifty metres below me in plain view. I was starting to unshoulder my rifle, estimating the pig was perhaps 200 metres off, when it suddenly shot across my bows followed a scant ten metres behind by Flash and Snow; silent as shadows and pushing hard to close the gap. One hundred metres further back old Bing was still letting me know he had put up an animal for the pack to chase, and eventually shot across the track too – out of the race now because of age.

I retired him on the spot and Flash took over within a very short space of time. I'm pretty sure there is even a subconscious "hanging-fire" in a capable up-and-comer, knowing the top dog would do the trick, a certain reticence to sneak off and find, maybe even deference to number "One". Better it is, once a young dog has been on a few pigs and understands it pleases the boss to catch one, to take it out by itself to where it is known half-grown pigs are in residence, and let it find and stop it's own quarry a few times. It won't be long before, even in the company of other members of the pack it'll do the same thing. Too often a young dog is hampered by lack of opportunity, out-gunned and out-classed by the more experienced of his kennel-mates.

Early in 1999 I was given Rebel as a six week old puppy by a very good mate of mine. I was actually given two pups but the female one was killed by my jealous bitch not long after the two pups were brought home. (Something to watch out for when introducing new girl-dogs to the pack). But Rebel thrived and became my mate, coming everywhere with me in the truck until about a year old when he had to learn to stay at home more often.

Cedric Fleming (my mate who had given me Rebel) kept two of the litter as well and named them Spark and Fly. They were obviously of whippet parentage and even the eye-dog ancestry showed through markedly. Not heavily built, they were all lean and more streamlined looking than the dogs I had traditionally run.

Rebel learned the ropes behind Rex, Blackie, Pongo, Kiwi and Bruiser, mostly in the thick stuff and occasionally in the "native", and shone at an unusually young stage. The first pig found by himself and stopped by himself was a creditable 90lb. boar and you can bet I made a real fuss of him on the spot. He never looked back from there and it was noticeable that he was a good deal ahead of his two litter mates. While they were keen and fast they hadn't yet cottoned onto the idea of finding their pigs in the scrub away from the boss, and it wasn't until we chewed the fat over why etc. that it dawned on us that they were hunting by sight. The reason became obvious straight away and we wondered why it had taken us so long to drop to it.

Seg had a considerable acreage of bush at the back of his farm and got a lot of enjoyment out of seeing the wild pigs coming out of an evening and foraging among his dairy cows, or yearlings etc.

A certain amount of grass went west of course, but what's that compared to the fun of watching one's favourite wild animal at play? In the winter however the piggies played diggies in the grass and that's when Seg got his doggies to chase the hoggies. And then when Spark and Fly, imitating their mum Tui, had glorious fun chasing the swine away back into the bush, and thus protected the boss' pasture. It only happened a few times before the young dogs got to know what was afoot and it was a case of "Yay, there they are again, them black things up on the hill, lets go." Fly would chase a boar downhill into the gully and Spark would veer off on a slightly smaller young sow. Yippety – yip, (hey this is fun). Next time Seg rushed down from the house and undid Tui the two learners would be leaping at their kennel doors and career away down the farm race. An occasional leap skywards would locate them black things for the youngsters and they would duck under the wire and home in on the unsuspecting porkers.

By the time Seg, Nigel and Brendon took them into the scrub to find a pig to chase, come summer, they were left wondering why their up and coming pig dogs kept so much at heel. Shouldn't they be out fossicking for pig sign or scent? Searching out some hidden quarry in the fern?

Yup! I guess you've guessed it. Sparkie and Fly were waiting to see the black things to chase, for the bosses to SHOW them the piggy-wigs. It all happened unplanned and was certainly inadvertent. So things changed forthwith, and the two later became quite adroit themselves and ended up regular pig dogs.

Rebel though was some months ahead, for he had learned early on to hunt himself and be away from me searching out and investigating every whim and whiff on the breeze. And while not being a long-distance finder, he could winkle them out plenty good enough for me. His ability to track down, or pick up air scent was quite marked, but the area in which he particularly shone was the way in which he stopped boars from getting away.

I've had a few back-enders in my time, but none as consistent as Snow of years ago and Rebel of more recent times. He knew just as well as Spark and Fly did too, what pigs looked like away over yonder as today would prove. It would be a new experience for both him and me in that he found his pig without going and searching for it.

The farmer's young worker and I got on pretty well as we both loved catching pigs, so quite regularly Wayne (he would be known in the Waikato as the "hairy") would advise me of the possible profitability of having a look out the back of the farm. Here it was bounded by Lands and Survey Department country; once settled but abandoned. Wi-wi, gorse and manuka were bidding fair to establish ownership again and had reclaimed many of the steeper faces and guts, even some of the easier country as well.

This day was fine and breezy, yet with lots of cloud. I should have been early I know but for some long forgotten reason, made a late start with Shiney, Tahi, Rebel and Bud. They were all keen and as soon as I let the dog-box door fly open, out they shot, only 200 metres from the heavy gorse. With "rip" collars on Rebel and Tahi, we set off along the creek edge until reaching the boundary fence, where we turned uphill hoping to skirt the yellow prickly stuff by hugging the wires. Beyond this was a broad ridge covered in old pasture and heaps of regenerating gorse, with some manuka thrown in as well. And beyond that again was a valley with a creek flowing over pebbles and stones at the foot of the far slope. Towards the lower end of both ridges and along the creek-bottom was home to a sow and young litter. Wayne had seen them fairly recently and I knew too of their residency hereabouts and was at pains to avoid them if I possibly could.

The uphill slope was initially fairly steep and I had to exert a good bit of energy, which to some extent occupied my mind along with watching for gaps or passage-ways in the gorse, keeping an eye on my footsteps and ducking under the overhanging macrocarpa branches.

The dogs weren't at heel all the time, which was to be expected and even desirable, and it was only when I had gained some height that I became aware that Tahi hadn't been seen for longer than was usual, so I stopped to wait a while. He duly turned up some five minutes later and I was relieved that he hadn't found that sow with young. I'm pretty sure he had been down across the creek for he was pretty wet, possibly some residual scent on the damp grass had lured him on. The considerable expanse of heavy gorse was ideal cover for our quarry, the bracken being very evident as well, and that along with the cutty-grass that was scattered throughout, made it very appealing as a place to bed down in.

With the four dogs at heel again I carried on climbing slowly northwards. The top was only a little way above me now. Skirting a small slip overgrown by short ferns then brought me to where the level ridge-top stretched away a good distance before turning right where the macrocarpa trees petered out.

Here it was that the sun broke out again. A massive grey cloud had obscured it for the last half-hour and I stopped to breathe more easily a short time, and thought how good it was to be alive and well, up in the hills and away from human habitation (there was only one corrugated shed a long way behind me). Sure an' all! It was simply marvellous! Gullies and hills everywhere, a high peak off to the right, green grass and scrub, and water in the creek bottom. I sat on a big wi-wi bush to gaze about and the three younger dogs came to receive a pat, or sit and push up against me. Rebel though just stood and continued to stare off towards Mangonui. I took no notice and was about to lie back when he stiffened up with ears cocked and tail erect. He stared even more noticeably than before, something over there apparently quite intriguing!

I squinted towards where he kept looking – and then I saw it! On the parallel ridge over the creek a black object was moving in and out of the gorse-plants and heading the same way as we were, "So that's what kept you so interested eh Tahi." I guessed. His foraging lower down a short while ago had undoubtedly alerted the pig (for such it was), which had probably waited till the coast was clear before quietly slipping away. Now I could see him vacating the area in a distinctly business-like manner, not galloping along but stepping it out quite briskly.

Rebel wasn't used to seeing the pig first and my "Soo! Soo!" was all it needed to have him off downhill, heading for where he had last seen the enemy. Mr. Pig was by now though another 200 metres along the ridge and I saw him/her disappear into a larger stand of gorse and lost sight of him.

Whether he'd seen me or the dogs I'll never know, but I guess he had for he was certainly on the move now. He appeared again on the same level but considerably further ahead crossing a small open patch and disappeared again.

Then Rebel came into view, but way back. He was going uphill and had nearly arrived at where the pig HAD been when first seen. Dumb dog! I was heading on an intercept course. Down and across to where I estimated the boar would be. Why couldn't Rebel deduce the same? Ah well.

Shiney, Bud and Tahi had picked up on the urgency and followed flat-out in the wake of the tan lead dog. Just before dropping too low to see where they were, I spied the three younger dogs momentarily, on the same track as Rebel and the pig, noses down and galloping along between clumps or stands of ti-tree and gorse. I just had to leave them to it, trusting in Rebel's ability to pull the pig somewhere ahead. If only he'd not lose it at some creek, or overshoot among stock – or whatever. I knew I had to hurry but nonetheless nurtured my crook ankle as best I could. The down-slope to the creek was over a million cattletracks, jarring my legs as I jolted to the water-course.

I had enough confidence in my dogs to spend time looking for a "dry-foot" crossing – you know – the anxious sort of confidence which I guess wasn't really confidence at all but just slightly better than wishful thinking. There was a crossing of sorts, kanuka trunks lay tangled at a corner with clumps of clay between and just showing above the water. This was a definite boon and I gingerly negotiated to the far side but then faced a vertical two metre bank. A couple of seconds later I had decided on a large gorse-stem as my means of acquiring higher ground and pulled myself – somehow (I was desperate and on adrenalin) up and onto the grassy terrace. More old-man gorse blocked my path and I must confess I lost all patience with it and attacked in grand kung-fu style. Biff

– bash – chop – slash – chop – chop and I was through (me and a few hundred prickles that is) and racing (well, trying to hurry) north again. You see, there was this confounded hill in front of me which didn't want to move, so I had to instead.

My run had subsided now to a vigorous walk, an occasional trot on a down-slope and a good few stops to listen. Somewhere ahead I hoped my dogs had closed the gap and were letting me know – but no barking was to be heard yet. I stumbled on following a sheep track now as I skirted around the side of several small ridges and gullies, listening and wheezing and listening again. It meant having to hold my breath so as not to be put off by the gasping for air that someone was doing.

Surely by now they had caught up. But he did have a pretty good head-start and knew he was being targeted. No doubt he had all stops pulled way out in his endeavour to make the main bush and was pushing it to the max.

Up above me was a large basin where a good ginger boar had eluded Shiney and Bud a year before. They had put him up off to my right at the base of a cliff where he'd had his bed in jumbled rocks and toi-toi. The cunning old codger had bolted downstream into a stand of fairly tall ti-tree and gorse, carried on round the spur and then shot directly uphill and into this basin. I was thrilled to see my two young dogs hard on his trail and possibly gaining on him though a good fifty metres behind yet. The devious swine knew a thing or two though re losing dogs and ran straight into a mob of goats, grazing the hillside at the far end of the hollow. Fair through the middle he went, scattering goats to left and right, then did a big "u-turn" and came barreling straight down onto his back-trail, turned right once more into the ti-tree and gorse and disappeared. Buddy and Shiney raced right through the fleeing goats, not even glancing sideways, and followed him round in his "U-ee" and came flat-out down to the ti-tree themselves and also disappeared. And a moment or so later I saw Mr. Pig shoot across the ridge lower down than where I was now standing and thence into more gorse and was lost. Bud and Shiney lost the trail, somewhere and never crossed the ridge but came to me five minutes later looking pleased with themselves even though they'd lost him. I was pleased too to have seen them completely ignore the goats to left and right, and stay with the pig all the way round the course.

Now as I faced the same basin I couldn't hear a thing. There were several ways he could have gone and I set about eliminating the least likely ones as I listened. I doubted very much that he'd climb the higher country to my left and ahead. This would have been really daunting for the pig, especially if at this stage he'd become aware that the dogs were after him. More likely he'd either break down into the gullies that were choked with dense scrub (and these both converged not far away) or he'd barrel around the hillside contour-wise, heading for the bigger patch of manuka that clothed the next 500 acres. I had wished I'd had my tracker with me but it was away being repaired so was reliant on ears and eyes, and that intuition that sometimes comes.

So while I wasn't convinced that he had gone that way, I did a contour-crossing of two smaller ridges and gullies and came to where the two young dogs had put to flight their ginger boar of previous encounter. But where now?

Nothing indicated the presence of duelling animals at all. On occasion a hawk might suddenly wing away above the bush, a cow spook, or sheep may be seen congregating nervously in some corner.

Even a hare racing off, a pheasant squawking, a sudden rolling of a rock on steep ground or the snapping of a branch have all at various times been ideal "give-aways". Now all was extremely quiet. The wind was almost still and the conditions were ideal for hearing dogs bailing at even a considerable distance.

And I did! Hear dogs bailing that is. And the distance was indeed considerable. Far up the distant slope barking could just be made out and it was hard to pin-point it's exact location. It seemed to come from scattered manuka where a wet patch spawned a small trickle of water. And what's more, it wasn't moving. If in fact it was the pig I'd seen scarpering before, then it was probably a boar with hooks and likely larger than the hundred-odd pounds I had estimated. Anything less would have been caught and squealling lustily by now so I was spurred on again.

I dropped straight down to the creek, having to negotiate many largish rocks and stones that had tumbled from a bluff beside me, careful in my added haste not to "rick" an ankle. I even scooped up a handful of water as I crossed over before beginning the long slog uphill.

Anxious all the time lest the bailing stop, I was pushing myself to the limit. I was already overtaxed coming out of that first creek, and I was thankful that the scrub wasn't really too thick in front of me. The gorse was just as sharp though and each little steeper incline, just as daunting for an old-codger like me.

But the barking was clearer now and still consistent. Rebel wasn't saying much but Tahi was sure kicking up a ruckus along with his black and tan "Buddy". Shiney, a bit quieter than the other two was nevertheless giving voice occasionally too.

Up ahead was a small flat piece of ground tucked into the hillside and this is where I came across the stand-off. That he hadn't broken and gone I'd been wondering about, but now understood all too well his preference for staying put. A muddy-coated black-bristled boar of about 140lb was sitting in a small patch of bog, bum in the mud, tusks facing his tormentors. Slightly above at about two metres, Rebel stood, unmoving but watching intently. And staring straight back, the boar slobbered and ground his tusks some more and some more. The continuous click-clack was ominous and intimidating in the extreme, and so Tahi and Bud were keeping their distance to his left and rear. Shiney, on the opposite side was in under some heavier gorse and kept away a couple of metres as well. The whole tableau was a definite standoff. Had I not come I don't know for how much longer the threat of the dogs would have kept him there, but found the answer to that after the boom of the gun ended the whole thing seconds later.

Mr. Pig slumped right over into his muddy puddle and I had to get my boots dirty getting near enough to drag him out onto firm ground. There I did the bleeding and gutting part of the operation and found why his running days were over. His legs and hocks, trotters and hams seemed pretty-well intact and could have carried him a long way yet, and after a blow like he'd had to refresh his lungs, should have done him proud for ages.

As I went to de-nut him last of all I found cause to look at Rebel lying now quite unconcernedly a few metres away and sighed contentedly to myself "aha-aha". The job was pretty-well done for me actually. One testicle was hanging right outside his scrotum (ball-bag) and was only attached by one thin cord. The other was half out and half in, and it was these Mr. Boar was protecting by staying firmly on his backside in the cool, cool mud. I've no doubt Rebel had caught him up well before the other dogs had arrived and had assailed the fleeing pig's rear end remorselessly until finally in desperation, and to quench the fire in it, he'd whirled to fight, only to have the fawn dog back right off. Away he'd run again, hearing the dreaded approach of the back-up hounds and gain 50 metres before that awful stabbing tearing pain came once more. Round he'd come again – and run a second or so hence as Rebel bored

The boar bailed in the creek.

in a second time.

And sooner or later the decision was made, at a wet and cold swampy piece of ground, to kill the dogs first, the brown one anyway. Rebel, wise in the ways of pigs had done his fighting and declined combat under the circumstances and simply backed off, the threat of his presence so near the family jewels enough to ensure the three arriving dogs could fight if they wanted to. But no. They too deferred to Mr. Pig and simply stood around and "talked" very loudly. The boss was coming and they were telling him where to come, and making sure he heard.

I carried him out, back down to the small creek from where Bud and Shiney had spooked the red boar a year or more ago, down through the tall manuka and scattered gorse and across some fairly swampy ground till at last I could leave it near a farm track and come back in my yellow Mitsi' L200. It weighed 129lb late that night and as I cut it up, still shook my head in admiration of Rebel's technique at pulling him up. Somewhere in his learning, as he followed escaping male pigs he'd discovered the best place to bite and ever after harried the same spot. Many more daddy pigs rued the day Rebel found them and at this stage I can recall only one ever getting away.

Seeing Is Believing

Kalvin rang late on a Friday night. It was August and still miserably cold and wet and I wasn't too sure whether I'd venture out tomorrow. The days of floundering around in sodden clothes and footwear just for the fun of it had somehow over the years lost it's content of fun so that it appeared to me now as simply floundering around just for "it". The idea that floundering around for "it" wasn't fun anymore had come gradually of course. Just part of growing older, wiser and "up" I guess. But Kalvin, being Kalvin, was just as enthusiastic as ever.

"What you got on tomorrow Reg?"

"Dunno! It's a bit wet isn't it?"

"Yeah! Na! I've got a good one lined up. We'll get him too I reckon."

"Actually--."

"Bring Rebel and Tahi and I'll meet you at Cooper's Beach. I've got this place where my mate from work hunts and he reckons there's a boar hanging about with the younger pigs he's seen. What time do you think we should meet?"

His eagerness had me feeling a bit mean as something else popped into my mind.

"I'm not too sure Kalvin. I mean, if this bloke's dogs can't catch the boar, what makes you think–."

"Na, na! He doesn't use dogs. He only goes with his .270 and waits on the hill for them."

"Oh, okay, how often has he seen this boar?"

"He hasn't."

"What? I thought you said he'd seen a good boar with some smaller ones, didn't you?"

"Well, yeah, na, he hasn't seen it- actually–he–um–he says he's seen these big marks on the track."

"Oh, right. And he reckons it's a good boar."

"Yeah!"

"Does he see the hoof-prints very often?"

"He's seen them once anyway and he says that--!"

"How many pigs has he actually got off this place?"

"Well–none– sort of . . . yet."

"But–?"

"Dad's going to come too. He's bringing Blue and his mate's got a couple of young dogs he wants to give a bit of practise to as well, and with your dogs there too we'll nail him for sure."

The nailing of "him", if "him" was there was definitely a drawcard I do admit. But Kalvin, me, his Dad, Dad's mate and thirty dogs I thought might be a bit much so I –

"My mate Serge is coming too with his rifle – just to make sure if we bail him – you know."

So now there'd be seventeen people, sixty-eight dogs and one "him". I raised my eyebrows to Olive as I listened to Kalvin trying his best to convince me. And in spite of the probable rain and the horde of hunters, I couldn't bring myself to be churlish and ended up agreeing to meet at seven at the corner.

The corner duly arrived in front of my windscreen bang on time, and there too were Brett and Paul Somers, and a stranger who had to be Serge,

After we had all said "gidday" and found out who each other was we started to discuss our chances as we looked anxiously at the sky and waited for Kalvin to turn up.

I knew Brett and Paul fairly well by now, having hunted with them on a few occasions, but had yet to get to know Serge so started with some safe questions.

"You hunted with Kalvin much before Serge?"

"No, not really. He's told me all about it though."

"Yeah, I can imagine." And so I could. When Kalvin gets started on boars and pigs and dogs and tusks, and kilos and kilometres, there's no stopping him.

"– but I've never seen dogs do it. A gun's pretty sure isn't it. More so than a dog don't you think? I mean, a bullet out of this machine and they're as dead as a dodo. No second chance, that's it! How can a dog compete with a bullet?"

"A bullet can't go and find a pig Serge, a dog can," I pointed out.

"Oh, for sure. But how can a dog produce 'knock-down' power like a gun? What if the big boar just decides to run away – what then?"

"'What then' is where those little white pointy things in the dog's mouth come into their own mate."

"What do you mean?"

"A good 'stopping' dog bites the pig's backside, his legs, his nuts. And keeps biting until the pig gets so annoyed or hurt that he stops and spins around to fight."

"And?"

"And the dog simply backs off and barks to let me and the other dogs know where he and the boar are."

"But what if he just won't stop for the dog?"

"Well then, that's where a really good dog comes into it's own. Can you imagine a savage dog having a go at your nuts as you ran away? What would you do? I reckon I'd sit down pretty smartly myself and try to protect them things."

"Do they actually do that?"

"Too right – well, some of the time anyway."

Kalvin arrived about then and climbed out apologising.

"Sorry you bunch. I didn't get to bed till 2am this morning. Just couldn't wake up. Sorry."

"She's right Kal," we all reckoned. "Let's get among it."

It turned out that the place we were going to wasn't where I thought it was at all, but several kilometres in a more southerly direction. But within a half-hour we all pulled into the long driveway that wound up a hill.

The ocean wasn't too far away and I could hear the booming of the breakers and smell the salt on the air; seaweed and sand and seashells sprang to mind too. The scent of them all was borne on the breeze, the leftover of last night's fierce wind and it's accompanying rain.

Just now though the sun shone through and it was really quite pleasant on top of the hill as we debated on who would go where and do what. Seeing as how this was Kalvin's spot I deferred to him and he deferred to his dad and his mate Paul.

They looked at the clouds still hurrying westwards and did some mental acrobats. They looked too at the bush-covered sides of the gullies west of here and pointed down the slope.

"We'll head down there Kalvin and come back along the gully to our right. That'll give us the wind off those faces there and give the dogs a bit of an advantage. You may spook a big one and push him over the ridge

Waiting for the bark. Paul Somers, author and Brett Roycroft.

our way – especially if he runs with the wind. That okay?"

"Yeah, yeah! Me an' Reg'll head along the ridge here and maybe look over there a bit." He pointed to a ferny, scrubby smaller ridge behind us. "Serge can come with us, eh Serge?"

This arrangement suited us all and was implemented forthwith, Brett and Paul moving away downhill. Kalvin, Serge and I waited a while, giving them a chance to get right down into the creek bottom before we began our search. Kalvin didn't have any dogs today and so for us three my four dogs would have to do.

In due course then Tahi and Shiney were allowed to start fossicking around and did so in the wake of Bud and Rebel. These last two had been inching away along the grassy ridge, stretching permission impatiently until I clicked my fingers and let them go. Twenty metres along the whole four had now turned straight down the hill and were last seen heading into some dead fern just on the far side of the swampy bottom.

Bud's bark a few seconds later took Shiney and Tahi poste-haste leftwards, the shaking fern telling us where they were headed. Rebel was apparently still further left again and unaware of the chase. Kalvin and Serge had both seen a boar crash down our side of the ridge and light out left – this only seconds after they heard it snort and Buddy bark. I wasn't paying attention and missed both.

"Good pig Reg," said Kalvin. "Not hanging about though."

"Any dogs after him?"

"Didn't see any, but probably – ah – listen!"

Tahi barked from well along the face. They were covering ground at quite a decent rate and angling up to go over apparently. Serge was waving frantically and pointing to the same spot as a couple of more barks came, this time from Shiney. Obviously the two dogs were pretty close and we were hoping they could stop the boar before he hit the road over the far side and disappeared up into the bigger pines.

Surely Rebel would have got in on the action. But we listened in vain for his voice for a good ten minutes and then resigned ourselves to failure again.

The returning dogs were given a pat for trying; Tahi, Shiney and Bud that is. Rebel was still away ten minutes later and we got to be wondering just where he was at.

"Any chance of that dog of your's catching it do you think Reg?" This from Serge as we mulled around on a gorsey knob, still looking hopefully towards the pines.

"Anything is possible Serge – though not probable after this length of time. If they don't stop him in the first five minutes, more than likely the thing will get clean away."

Brett and Paul were still away on their circuit somewhere and we decided to wait where we were for them to appear, probably, we guessed coming down this ridge we were on. We hadn't heard anything of them in the intervening time either. Maybe we could have heard one of their dogs barking even against the wind but nothing had transpired.

We sat down in some long kikuyu after a while but didn't stay there very long. A dog barked away down towards where Brett and Paul ought to be and we all stood up. So too did my three dogs, and a second later shot off lickety-split for the distant barking.

"Doesn't sound like one of Dad's dogs Reg," said Kalvin as he peered away towards some taller ti-tree.

"No, that's Rebel all right. He's got a long way down from where we last saw him. No wonder he didn't home in on that boar back there."

A squeal a few minutes later took Kalvin and I down into the scrub and heading towards what turned out to be a sixty-pound sow. It was caught in some pretty open kanuka and despatched for humane reasons straight away. Some swampy ground had probably hindered her flight somewhat and allowed Rebel to catch up and arrest her. Now as we retraced our steps across that same swampy ground one of Brett's dogs came to us and stayed a few minutes. They couldn't be too far away we guessed, but still didn't meet up with them for another half-hour. During this time Kalvin had lugged the sow up to Serge and I had gone crashing away down another face to put paid to another sixty-pounder, a small boar that had tried to bail in a terribly thick patch of fern and devil-weed. He was doomed from the time Bud searched him out of course and the thicket he died in only enhanced his life span a couple of minutes at the most. It was my turn to carry now and by the time I met up with Serge and Kalvin, Paul and Brett were there too. Being empty-handed and seeing our two small pigs made them keen to try a bit longer so it was decided we'd head across the road where the bigger boar must have gone.

And this is where my memory lets me down a bit. I can't remember which way Paul and Brett went. Maybe this was another day and they weren't even there – I'll have to check with Kalvin!

Anyway, this particular foray across the road saw my four dogs catch another small pig mere metres above it, which was killed and left until later, hidden under some ponga branches.

Now Kalvin, Serge and I wandered up a climbing track under the pines heading roughly north-east. I knew this place from years ago when I hunted here regularly and pointed out where I had caught a 140-pounder way back then. I know Pinto Dangen got a good boar from hereabouts those days too, winning a competition with it that weekend.

While there was plenty of under-shrubbery and prunings to hide in, I reckoned the virgin scrub through the fence on our left was a more likely haven for any pork in the vicinity. Still, we carried on.

Eventually Serge and Kalvin left me to search further along by myself. I had to come back the same way anyway so they opted to wait where they were. Another 300 metres though convinced me to turn back too. With no sign of pig-tracks, rooting, tree-rubbings or wallows, it was debatable whether any perseverance would produce the result we wanted. Besides, the denser scrub over to the right now, I reckoned was well worth checking out. Thus thinking, I started back and sauntered slowly downhill to where I had left the others. Only they weren't there. Maybe they were through the fence too. So I climbed over where a pig-run, not recently used, ventured underneath the wire.

There was a lot of devil-weed underfoot now, but it's easy enough stuff to get through and I forged ahead. Some sign was evident here and my expectations went up a notch. Rebel wasn't often seen, Tahi either along with Shiney, and only Bud stayed at heel.

It wasn't long before the ground became quite steep and I worked my way gradually uphill and about a quarter of the way across the face. Looking away down towards the road I could see the occasional vehicle drive by as well as my truck parked up in the farmer's paddock. No sign now of the others. I pushed on for ten minutes and found all four dogs had returned at once. "Aw, bust it", I thought and turned around to head back. The wind had dropped away to almost nothing at this stage and I was fairly warm as I worked slowly back towards the fence. The rocky ground underfoot meant I had to be careful placing my feet to save twisting an ankle. Not much enjoyment would have been derived had I done so and I was happy to mooch carefully along.

A gorse prickle in my knee was annoying me, and not paying proper attention, I tripped on a larger branch and fell headlong into a seemingly solid phalanx of others. Luckily not one found a resting place in my face or neck, but one or two did find my lower arms. I was busy extracting myself when Rebel chose to bark again from some way below me. And I realised then that I was on my own.

Shiney, Bud and Tahi had all been swallowed up by the scrub some couple of minutes ago but now let me know where they were. Down there with Rebel, all four were seemingly hot on the trail of a good pig, for all were sounding off from time to time. The pig, for pig it could only have been went downhill and around to the right.

I listened. A bark! Only one dog close up now and it seemed they had climbed and were opposite me across the steep face. Then no more. The waiting with baited breath lengthened and stretched until I blew hard and listened again. Nothing!

I turned to head back when five long minutes had gone by. The dogs would arrive shortly I knew. No sense in wasting time. Back I went, past an unused wallow, climbing slightly, gorse-bashing a bit and was only twenty metres from the fence when a giant "hullaballoo" erupted almost under my nose.

I had subconsciously heard an animal (dog, I thought) pushing hurriedly through the short scrub to my right and aiming to bump into me in a few metres. Then a couple of barks and an enraged snort told me the dog had been on a pig, it being chased by a bevy of hyped-up hounds haring hurriedly, helter-skelter hither and thither in his wake, harassing his heavy hairy hinder parts, hammering his hocks, hampering and

I dumped the boar over the top wire and let it fall.

hurting as they hunted him down. Until at last he snorted "enough is enough", and turned to do battle, and high on adrenalin they "had at" the harried hog. The "hurly-burly" was horrendous. One hound hung back, hugging the ground as he hunkered down. And a second later launched himself for that left-hand haunch and hung on. I heard the whole thing, the "hands-on" happening just below me, the hum and din of the warfare until habit took over and I, as humanely as possible made him history.

He was only about 100lb I thought but had given a pretty good account of himself nevertheless. Several small pokes and gashes were sported by Shiney, and Tahi had a small piece of skin hanging off his flank. The short tusks of their adversary had indeed taken their toll but none were life-threatening and I gave them all a pat and made quite a fuss of them for a few minutes.

Then came the homework. Gutting, tying up to carry, and the carry itself took about fifteen minutes and on arriving at the fence only a short way ahead, I dumped the boar over the top wire and let it fall. Down the track a hundred metres I saw Kalvin slowly working his way back up to where I was. It was his dad's dog Ringo who had appeared as I stuck the pig and no doubt he had heard the ruckus as well and was coming to lend a hand.

Kalvin and Reg.

"Good on you Reg. Hey, Serge would love to see that wouldn't he." He was referring to the boar's nuts hanging in, but only just. The ball-bag (scrotum) was clearly ripped and torn, almost as if a knife had done the job afterwards. But I knew whose teeth had inflicted those nasty wounds. Kalvin took some photos and away we went down to show Serge.

"I never really doubted you you know Reg. But seeing certainly is believing." This with his backside pressed firmly up against the truck while he kept a weather-eye on Rebel.

First Law Of The Musket

I was to run foul of the above mentioned law on a day that left me ruing my actions considerably. It was a day spent hunting by myself, keeping my own company and talking only to Reg! I enjoy being alone in the bush sometimes but generally prefer to have company, especially that of another hunter and there again, one with a dog or two. Having two packs along has never been a handicap to me other than on two occasions. Dogs most often get along okay if handled the right way. I've never allowed my dogs to fight and consider anyone with the mentality encompassing "my dog can fight your dog" as being a stupid idiot. Dogs are there to fight pigs if they are pig dogs, and ought to have had it knocked into them which species of animal is lawful game. However, I know (from experience) that now and again you'll get a dog with that tendency towards wanting to be "cock-o-the-hoop". This aspiring alpha-male (in my pack anyway) knows that in actual fact he is not the alpha-male at all – I am! But the wish is in the back of his mind and on meeting other dogs, may surface in that strutting around which becomes growling then snarling and then, if not checked, fighting. I find it advantageous, if two of us are going out together with two packs to let my mate get his dogs out to scamper about, especially if we are in my area, while my dogs remain in their box as I don my apparatus. When gun, bullets, knife, camera and string are attached, boots laced up, clothing adjusted etc, I get my mate to hang back a moment with his pack. I walk a short distance along the track, he opens my dog box and I immediately call my hounds to heel and keep slowly walking. He catches up gradually by which time the dogs are almost settled to hunting and not worrying about territory or ascendancy.

There was a time my main dog thought he was the pack-leader and I had to deal with it forthwith when it became apparent. I had at the time

74

two communal kennels like chook-pens. Two dogs lived harmoniously in one four by two metre mesh wire cage which had sleeping quarters extra again. Through the joining door lived three dogs in the same conditions. Fred, Yellow and Blackie got on wonderfully together and I had no trouble at all until this particular day. They lived mainly on Tux dog biscuits at the time; Blackie being given his in the far corner, Yellow's were thrown inside the sleeping box and Fred would wait, even though he was a lot bigger than the other two while they were apportioned their rations, and receive his last as I exited the gate. But fairly frequently I liked to vary their menu and give them milk, dead animals which had been cut up or dog-roll, even a change of dog-biscuit brand to break the monotony. Now, I love jelly, but if I had to have it everyday I'm sure I'd get sick of it after a time.

Today I had chunks of beef from a Hereford which had broken it's hip. I threw Blackie her piece in the far corner and immediately Fred growled and leapt for it, shoving Blackie aside. I growled at him but he simply ignored me, leaping into the sleeping box still with Blackie's meat.

"OK" I thought, "I'll give Blackie yours" and did so. Out shot Fred and grabbed that too, just missing my boot as he leapt back inside. I was so furious now, and yelling at Fred to "come here you mongrel sod," I reached in and grabbed his tail. He didn't want to come out though and I had to exert all my energy before I finally got him outside, the meat still firmly clamped in his mouth.

"Let go Fred, let go!" I commanded still hanging on to his tail.

All he did was growl and pull strenuously for the opening to the box.

I was pretty worked up by now and fortunately recognised what I was up against right away. Had I let Fred get away with it I'd never again have him under my command or authority. I knew instinctively that I had to get the better of him and win this battle. So I grabbed the meat in his mouth and began a tug-of-war. He growled and pulled, growled and yanked and finally let go and latched onto my arm. I didn't even feel it. With adrenalin pumping I attacked him and threw him on the concrete, one knee on his neck and my fist hammering his head. Up he got, down he went again, this time with his teeth in my other arm. I kicked him and punched him, throttled him and yelled at him and tried strangling him again. More little marks appeared on my hands and arms and blood was everywhere but I daren't let up. On it went for another full minute and

I was almost exhausted. He could hardly breathe so with one almighty effort I yanked him up and threw him through the dog box door and kicked the wood behind him. I hurt my foot but I didn't care. No meat was touched for a good hour as far as I could ascertain. Even Blackie and Yellow seemed cowed.

My arms and hands were a mess and I should really have had a doctor look at them. A hot half hour soak in the bath, quite a bit of sticking plaster and a determination to ignore the pain saw me through. About an hour later I went outside to see what's what. Blackie and Yellow sat beside their meat which was untouched and Fred was sill inside where I had last seen him. Patting Yellow I picked up her meat and speaking kindly to her gave it into her mouth. Instantly she fell on it voraciously and I had to do the same to Blackie. She wagged her tail to say thank-you and got stuck into hers pronto too. Next I called "Fred, here Fred, c'mon old chap, dinner time," in as friendly a voice as I could put on and chucked his hunk inside with him. I went to bed feeling pretty sore believe me and in the morning went outside to see how things were.

Well "things" were back to normal, absolutely. Fred was truly pleased to see me and wagged his tail saying "hello." And never bothered me or his mates rations again. As far as his aggression towards me and the other dogs was concerned, you'd think yesterday never happened. Perhaps he had learnt his lesson as was intended and I was once more leader of the pack.

The two occasions on which having another hunters dogs along didn't work out went like this. We were walking alongside a river, skirting a flat paddock where some sheep were grazing. All went well until about halfway around when one of my mates dogs set out after a woolly by itself in a hollow of the meadow. Another of his dogs hared off to lend a hand and then another.

"You'd better run and get your dogs off Len, (not his real name). I can't lest my dogs think it's "all on". Hurry up, go go go!"

He ran all right but it was too late for the thin skinned Romney ewe and when I arrived at a controlled leisurely walk with my dogs tight at heel, I had to cut it's throat. Now what to do? It had spoiled our day right at the start and we both felt gutted. (The sheep probably did too) So being only a short distance from the truck I went back, retrieved a pencil and a piece of loo paper and wrote a note, leaving it on the carcass under a stone "See you on the way back, Reg." What we got on our foray into the scrub I can't remember and on the way home, called at the farmer's place, made my apologies, inquired after the price of sheep and promised to come back tomorrow with the money. He knew me fairly well and graciously acceded. What's more, he never held it against me as well he might, and I still hunt his property from time to time. Even though it wasn't my dogs doing the damage I thought it better to be seen as responsible and happily parted with the going rate.

The other episode happened on the way back from our hunt around the back of Taratara. I had a 90lb boar on my back and as I tripped over at a fence, suddenly found myself in the middle literally, of a ten animal dog fight. Ken, Johnny and Evelyn all pitched in to establish law and order, but it took a while. Miraculously I never got so much as a scratch, the dogs being much more concerned in detaining the escaping pig, or claiming ownership of the same and I suspect the former deteriorated into the latter.

Today though, I was by myself apart from Tahi, Bud, Shiney and Rebel. I was feeling lucky too, don't ask me why. I suppose a brilliant May morning coupled with the form the pack was showing of late, and a healthy tax refund last week had me brimming with confidence. I knew there was a good boar in the vicinity because several times over the last few weeks I had cut his sign wandering all over. It didn't take me long to decide I was in the middle of his territory and this was now the third time I was trying very hard to run him down.

Another hunter had taken a good pig out of here recently, but that was further to the left of where I reckoned my boar hung out much of the time. At 120lb the one caught was maybe a bit too light to be the one I was after and I had decided this pig was going to bow out in the next week or so, riding the back of my "Mitsi".

You can be sure I had my Rossi .44 magnum over my shoulder at this time as I might need it, (hoped I would anyway). The thing is, I forgot all about the "NEVER" rules. These of course originated on the American Frontier in the times of Daniel Boone and Simon Kenton. Those days they had muzzle-loading flintlock rifles and needed them frequently in protection against the Red Indians. There were no such things as lever-action, pump-action or even bolt-action rifles, let alone anything resembling a semi-automatic. When a shot was fired, it was imperative one stopped all else and saw to the reloading sequence post-haste, pronto and forthwith, immediately straight away with no time wasted right now. Get it? Until your gun was loaded, powder in and ball rammed home with that ramrod you were almost as vulnerable as you could get. All those frontier men had this law drilled into them before they were out of nappies even, and never forgot it! It's companion rule governs the whereabouts of the firearm when away from home. It states that when going into the woods, any person at all, always carries their gun with them and never allows it out of arm's reach. Even at night the gun/rifle is kept right alongside, loaded. If a pistol is owned, it is put under one's pillow for instant use if need be.

I read, or heard of (can't remember which now) an episode in the life of either Daniel Boone or Simon Keaton (can't remember that now either) relating to this maxim.

The intrepid frontier man (whichever it was), was known to be very fleet of foot and owed his life to this very fact early one morning. He was out in the woods and camped down for the night. No fire was lit for the area he was in was crawling with either Wynandot or Shawanoe Indians and this would have drawn them to himself like a beacon. He was relatively untroubled though as he lay down to sleep. Many nights such as this he had spent under the stars in the new world forests, so, having found a secluded dell well off the beaten track, he hoped, he put his musket alongside his bed and was soon in the land of Nod.

In the early hours of the morning despite being a light sleeper, he was discovered by a roving band of Indians. One of their number had literally almost stepped on him, froze on the spot, and sized up the situation in a second. He could see the frontier man's rifle alongside him, and slowly, ever so slowly, inched forward and cautiously withdrew the weapon, never making the slightest sound. Next he backed off a wee way, and using that peculiar method of communication the Red Indians had perfected called in the others of his band. A bird's call, very low, but repeated twice at frequent intervals had ten of his brother warriors with him within a minute or two.

Apprising them of the situation, they encircled the sleeping scout, someone accidentally on purpose snapping a stick when they stood in a circle around the still sleeping man.

Simon (I've decided it was him) was awake right then, but kept his eyes shut and felt surreptitiously for his rifle, only to find it gone. You can imagine his alarm on finding himself unarmed and surrounded by his bitter enemies. But he immediately played on the Indians well known admiration of bravery, and leaping to his feet started laughing his head off, and holding out his hand in congratulations, began going around the circle, shaking hands with each one of his fully armed captors. As

78

a cat plays with a mouse, so the Red men humoured their prisoner. He kept laughing uproariously, slapping them on the shoulder, and coming to the last in the circle, put out his hand again. As the bemused warrior clasped his hand (as they had seen the white men do) he found himself yanked off his feet and catapulted forward onto his face. Keaton leapt over him and was gone, dodging through the trees, running like he'd never run before. There were whoops of outrage and bloodthirsty yells and screams as they all lit out after him. But they never had a chance. He lived to lay low many more redskins thanks to his supreme fleetness of foot and cool nerve in adversity. His only regret was having to purchase a new rifle to replace the one the Wyandots or Shawanoes (can't remember which now) now possessed.

Now what's the moral of that story? There ain't no Red Indians out in the bush to worry about yet the adage remains just as true today. "Never let your weapon out of your sight" – that's the one I forgot.

We were approaching a point in the forest road where it goes up and over a spur turning a right-hand corner at the same time. Where the pine trees hadn't been planted was all shortish ti-tree and I usually stand on the corner high point and scan the countryside for whatever. The next ridge over, some years ago was manuka and grass and it was here I saw around 30 pigs one late afternoon. They were working their way out of the scrub, trotting and walking and nosing about, oblivious to the fact that I was watching them! Two good boars and two lesser ones were among the sows and weaners but I didn't see any really young suckers and I surmised that some of that thirty-odd were still resident hereabouts. And one of those four boars was probably the owner of those large hoofprints that had me hopeful this morning in the autumn of '05.

Tahi was absent and had been for a quarter of an hour. I had noticed him being interested in something a while back where a side track branched off uphill. He got very keen and dashed about for half a minute and then went over the side with his nose in the air. Shiney followed and returned almost immediately to walk behind again, whereas Bud and Rebel had only just come back from some foray of their own in the opposite direction. Pig-marks were not abundant but seen here and there enough to keep me buoyed-up, hopeful of a strike at some time soon.

I waited now at the high point for Tahi. As number two dog he was expected to do his share of the finding, and often did, so it was with high hopes I sat down on the hard clay to await developments. There was no breeze to talk about and at nine o'clock the sun was warm and shining directly into my eyes. If it hadn't have been for the prospect of a chase presently, I might have gone to sleep quite easily, and as it was I got to the drowsy stage.

I came instantly awake though at Tahi's "pig-alert" call. Somewhere near the swampy creek directly in front of me his bark rang out and drew the three remaining dogs in a hurry over the side. The chase, when next I heard of it, was upstream a good distance, being executed still by Tahi alone. That the other three were trying hard to catch up I didn't doubt, and even told myself that it had to be a reasonable size to be moving so far so fast.

It must have out-run the brindle lead dog somewhere about there, for I heard no more. Bud came back fairly soon, then Rebel and Tahi together, a minute before Shiney. I called Tahi over and gave him a pat just to show him I was pleased with his efforts. He understood too, and immediately headed back down to where he had been. Silly dog probably expected the pig to return for another round of catch-me-if-you-can. He was certainly a tryer and of my present pack puts more energy into finding than any other. The other three didn't share his optimism though and hung about until he returned, panting a little but still looking business-like at a fast trot. And even as he arrived he stopped, and again looked over his shoulder towards the swampy creek.

I got up and started off towards where the road dipped into a hollow in the shade of the big pine trees. Just as I stepped across a muddy patch with water trickling through, a late morepork shot across in front of me and alighted in a dead pine a few metres away.

His owlish stare fixed on my face, and I thought of the saying that suggests the seeing of a morepork during daylight hours meant a death was imminent. Was it true? Did it really work that way? Whose death was it staring at me about? But I wasn't superstitious – was I? I put it out of my mind and carried on along a small flat and began climbing a rocky rise.

Here and there on this road was evidence of a big boar. The same one as I had noticed regularly over the last month or two. Still about, possibly even not far away, this being his territory was imbued with a lingering presence of danger and excitement. The thrill of the chase was here somewhere, waiting. And in spite of myself my heart-rate was raised just a mite and my ears were working overtime, deciphering the myriad noises wafting on the breeze. Rustlings and cracklings as the dogs returned and vanished were heard ahead of the wind sighing in the boughs and branches of the pines. A heavy "plop" in a water-hole registered too, and the cawing of a magpie, while noticed, weren't really heard at all. These extraneous sounds were simply "background," but not what I strained to hear.

Then a bark came, loud and repeated, a good distance ahead. A few more came, and then a flurry of yapping and hollering and my reflex action of running frantically uphill was extant right then. The farmer was moving his sheep. He might have told me he was mustering this morning. I could have informed him of my intended hunt for the big boar and he may have postponed his stock work until the afternoon. Not likely though eh! It was really only a minor inconvenience and didn't bother me too much to be honest. The only danger being that a young dog might home-in on the barking and make a nuisance of itself. But there was no likelihood of that today. After a short while in the team the younger dogs get to know the voices of their pack-mates and under good discipline aren't tempted to rush off to a stranger's bark.

Might be a good idea to sit and wait a while anyway – give the man a chance to finish his chores and move on. It wasn't likely any pig in the vicinity would be spooked by farm dog's barking, they pretty soon get to know the difference between round-up barking in the paddock and the "on my trail" exuberance of a finder getting close. By the time a pig has matured to 100lb plus, one living in the proximity of farmland will have figured it all out pretty competently and not be phased by the workings of heading dogs and huntaways.

Even so I continued waiting where I was. This was my day of relaxation (when I wanted to) – and I wanted to right now. It was good finding a gorse-free spot to sit down on where I could see out over the scrub. This was where Eric Schultz and I, years ago, had hunted down the ridge in front of me to find my dog Sue with a punctured lung, and a few minutes later bag the black and white dog-killer of Mt Knobby (*Diary of a Pig Hunter* page 83). Other pigs too had been accounted for hereabouts, some good ones among them and I was hopeful of another today. Even a good chase would be exciting. Both Rebel and Tahi were likely to come through for me in the finding of my boar (I was already thinking of it as such) and Shiney too was no slouch there either. Buddy even did it occasionally, so as I got to my feet after half an hour I was still pretty high on expectations and sauntered off along the track again. With no time limit on me and a pig likely in the area, going slowly forwards gave the finders time to explore every whim that came their way. I've seen dogs looking keen in some direction, only to chuck it in as I move on. Better it is to let them decide whether what they suspect is enough to draw them off into the scrub, or whether the signals they are receiving are not strong enough and they turn away.

I shouldered my rifle as Buddy fell in beside me and led off along the track. Ahead of us now was a hillside above the road covered in manuka and all the attendant subspecies of coprosmas, hebes, gorse and flax, pittisporums and rewarewa. My favourite among the lower storey shrubs is the mingi-mingi with it's pretty light green leaves and there were good numbers of these beautiful little trees scattered throughout.

The road dipped as it turned a corner, small rocks and stones evident where the rainwater had washed the clay away. Shiney put her nose in the air and stopped. A slight breeze came off the hill just then and brought something of interest to the white bitch. She waited another moment and then turned away. Rebel also, after watching her scanning the scrub lost interest at the same time. It was Buddy in fact who lead off at a run. Rebel looked over his shoulder, froze and bolted too. All four dogs had assaulted the steep track and disappeared straight up the hill. Was he here after all?

Within twenty seconds I knew. A shindig broke out fifty metres away and told of a number of dogs rarking up a pig close by. The absence of any squeal brought the heart-rate up again, likely it was a boar facing the dogs up there and I unslung my .44. On the point of leaping up the bank myself, the squeal came loud and clear, a heavy squeal admittedly and I dropped (placed) my gun on the ground and turned again to the scrub. It only took a few moments to home in. I was anxious to save the sow unnecessary torture and fought vigorously uphill.

Backed into a flax bush but held securely was indeed a sow. She fought savagely and used her weight (about 90lb) to throw the dogs around a bit but was doomed regardless. In the open now, away from the flax bush I was able to grab her tail and get her on her side. Still, she didn't like it and struggled strenuously, kicking and heaving about in her endeavour to free herself.

My shouted commands of "let go, let go" finally got through to the dogs, and as one they disengaged. Bud and Tahi needed further admonition for a minute or two until they realised that it was all over for them this time. They loved to nip in from behind me and got just one bite in before having to leap away from my stick, but they finally left me

Willie Presow letting a large sow have her freedom.

to it. A string now tied the pig's legs together and she was left lying on her side but attached to a manuka trunk. Next I called the dogs in turn, looped a string over their heads and hitched them to some other tree or shrub. In a short while all five were secured, four dogs and one pig, all tied to their respective tree-trunks and branches.

Now the good part started. I untied the string holding the sow to the ti-tree, and keeping my knee on her neck and her top front leg pulled back along her flank, slipped the remaining string off her limbs. All I had to do next was point her in the right direction downhill, let go and leap away. On several occasions though this plan has come unstuck and the pig has turned on me for another go. Ingratitude seems to be common in our wild swine and you have to step lively sometimes. However, this broken-coloured sow must have been thankful and immediately took to her scrapers. Down she went and I could hear her hit the road some way below where I had left the rifle. The dogs didn't think much of my scheme though and tugged at their strings, whining a little as they watched their prize get away.

Ten minutes were allowed to go by before I could safely untie my hunting dogs now. And a strict eye was kept on them, particularly Tahi and Bud. Shiney and Rebel seemed to know the score and appeared to accept the present status-quo. Given the slightest encouragement though and they'd be away on her trail again in a flash. I was happy to think of her litter being reared to act as quarry next year or the following one. Another boar or four to chase would be a boon, and a sow or three to breed up yet more pigs was what it was all about and what was necessary if there are to be pigs around in the future.

I picked up my knife and gathered up the string and turned to go.

"Here Bud, here Bud, leave it alone now," I said as the black and tan hunter began heading away again.

"Good boy Tahi. Here Shiney, Rebel."

I was aiming for where I had left the road and angled down to come out right at the corner. As I did so Rebel had his nose to the ground and was burning up pace away from me opposite to where the sow had gone. Bud too was haring after him, then Tahi. I scratched my head and looked down. And bent down lower still. My rifle was lying on its side, sling extended, and imprinted in the clay inside the sling were two very large boar marks, canted over where he had been leaning into the corner. Obviously he had been with the sow, waited to determine which way the dogs would go and lit out for the horizon once this was established. Leaping off the bank, he landed alongside the gun and immediately turned, stepping inside the sling and leaving his heavy hoof prints to tease me.

Had I waited only a few more seconds and kept my rifle in my hands, no doubt I would have been presented a fine opportunity to bag the big fellow as he was getting away. The first law of the musket "keep it in hand and ready" was ignored and I missed out. But never mind. I've seen his sign a few times since and confidently expect one day to make his acquaintance a bit more intimately.

Corn On The Cob

The clouds I'd seen earlier had massed and thickened and the leaves were starting to rustle in the gum-trees overhead. And the breeze seemed to strenghten even as I picked up my pace, heading for the truck and home. Rebel and Bud, Tahi and Shiney scampered on ahead as I climbed out of the river depression and they saw the ute parked under the totaras near the crossing. Even they seemed to understand rain was in the offing and were looking to hop up inside their dog-box where they'd be warm and dry. Crossing the river had cooled them down, for they had just returned after yet another futile chase, trying to pull a pig I had known about a good while. I had exercised this particular hog a few times now and had been hopeful that today would at last see the dogs get the better of him. Wasn't to be though.

Just on daylight we had crossed the river, me carrying my gumboots and socks, slipping and sliding and "ouching" my way gingerly across the swollen torrent. It was up to me knees in the shallow place I often used to get to the scrub behind Wes' place. Dogs were out of their depth today of course but readily took to the water and ended up somewhat downstream, to come back trotting and shaking water off themselves, then trotting off again. I had used an old rag I carried as a ribcage wiper to dry my feet before slipping my socks on again, and then stuffed it into the bum-bag for later on. I had learned this trick as a result of using my singlet too often, and getting growled at by Olive.

"Why don't you take a rag specially to do that and keep your singlet dry," she had suggested.

I must have been a bit grumpy because I muttered something about "just one more thing to carry" and got out of earshot. However, next time I went hunting I remembered, conceded it was a good idea actually, and ever since have carted a piece of cloth for this purpose!

Having caught and gutted an animal I would generally leave it's back end intact until after the carry, simply to act as a reservoir, catching and pooling any blood that might (and most often did) accummulate as time progressed. And as occasion allowed, I would turn it right way up to drain a while and then use this rag to wipe around, which would leave very little mess and save my back, singlet and shirt getting all sticky and "yukky" from the carry.

So, boots on again, we had headed across a low swampy flat, aiming to hit the toe of a spur where ponga prevailed as cover and gave easier walking. All across the spongy water-logged ground, dense wi-wi thickets and masses of "wait-a-while" hampered progress, for me anyway. The bush-lawyer as I called it, or barrister as Big Ray Murray did seemed to have taken over this whole area and try as I might, never could find a clear path through. Billows upon billows of the stuff festooned every cabbage tree, gorse bush and manuka that ever grew hereabouts and I generally stayed on the "path" I had pushed and hacked through the middle.

Rebel and Co. were quite busy today. I knew we were in pig country of course and was pleased to see runways and pig-passages reasonably churned up by traffic. Pigs of all sizes had passed by in the recent past, one big fellow among them, my "rendezvous" pig I hoped.

We toiled all morning up to the skyline, along to the pines on the right, even over into the next gully, and back again through tight rubbish, open rubbish, steep faces, easy ridges, all to no avail! Till practically noon.

I was heading back towards the river, slightly despondent and watching Tahi poking about beneath some dying fern. A few metres away Buddy was doing the same and Shiney had come to see what they were up to. There was a yip from Tahi, a yelp from Shiney and they were off, flat-out back the way we had come, Buddy burning up ground a few metres to the rear. And just in front, a black and ginger boar of about 70lb was hot-footing it for somewhere far away.

Gone almost immediately from sight, I could tell where progress was by the sometimes "yip" from one or more of the hounds. But all went quite fairly quickly and peace reigned again. I sat and waited. Watching a stick-insect climb and then descend a dead ti-tree, and put out his front legs in an effort to gain another alongside, kept me occupied until the dogs turned up. Rebel was with them when they did, and so was a 70lb ginger and black boar. He wasn't a willing party to the get together though, and it was his complaining voice that called me from my reverie just fifty metres above them.

I had got past my stick-insect interlude and was on my feet scanning the manuka heads for a gecko, intent on seeing a little green fellow sunbathing and was only a few metres from the fern that had hidden the youngish pig twenty minutes before. No sound had been heard in all that time and I was totally absorbed in my fauna hunting until his shrill squeal told me what was afoot.

I got down there pretty fast and dispatched the half-grown thing and eventually slung it over my head and shoulders and departed for the river crossing. The unlucky pig on my back must have done a big circle and been heading back when he had run perhaps into Rebel. The others, still on his trail but behind far enough so they weren't barking would have materialised in no time flat and beaten me there. Not the rendezvous I was anticipating, or really wanting; Evelyn was due up today and would relish taking bush-pork home to Whangarei – exit pig.

So, here I was, having just recrossed the river. The L200 across the paddock was indeed a welcome sight for me too, and one more look at the sky towards the horizon told me. Yeah! Rain in the offing. But not just yet. The clouds, now black and covering the whole of the northern sky, were full of water and sometime soon, would empty out over the land before heading out to sea again.

I hurried on and dumped my burden on the tray, shut the dog-box and drove off, up a small incline and over some more grass to the gate and had to turn sharp onto the road. A grey double-cab Hilux had pulled up and not left me much room to turn. Then John put his head out of the window and said: "Good-day Reg, how'd it go?"

I pointed backwards onto the deck and smiled "howdy".

"You got one eh, good on you. I wish it had been on my place though."

He was my neighbour, not nextdoor really, but nextdoor to nextdoor neighbour. He and his wife owned the next block along, and were up from Wellsford to check on things for the weekend. They had been in to Mangonui for some supplies and were heading to the property now.

I explained that the pig I was carrying away probably had been on his/their place, only having to cross the river at any one of the dozen shallow fords to forage on his pasture.

"It's not my ruddy pasture I'm worried about," he replied. "The __ __ _____ pigs have been raiding my maize and making a confounded nuisance of themselves and a real mess. Can you help you reckon? Give them a boot up the backside, any side, anywhere?"

"Yeah, I'll have a go. I'll pop around after lunch and have a look eh?"

"Yeah, yeah, good man. I'll see you then eh." And he drove off all smiles, a thumb in the air.

The dogs had a sleep, I had a feed and the truck had another rest. I had another look at the sky and then had a second thought about heading around to John's place. Those clouds had piled up yet more and now were nearly here, a half-hour I reckoned at the most and there'd be wet stuff hanging about. Maybe I could have a yarn and promise I'd go tomorrow, or next weekend – I didn't fancy getting soaked – not after all that effort, keeping my feet dry – twice. And keeping my back dry once!

Fat chance!

"Howdy! You had your lunch? That didn't take you long – must be keen eh. Man, I'm pleased you came. There'll be nothing left by next weekend. Just as well we bumped into you I reckon. Come and have a look and see what you think."

Well, I already knew what I was thinking! Feet up, slippers on, tele going or a good book – "cuppa" perhaps.

I followed him up the rise to where he had his maize stacks. Toni and Cushla stayed back at the tent doing whatever it was they were when I had pulled up, but Ryan came for a walk with us. He was about 13 I reckoned, fair hair, sturdy build and a ready smile, he'd make a good pig hunter one day if they moved up here as planned. Between now and then they were getting ready to go free-range chook farming and the river-flat of maize they had harvested was meant to be the mainstay of feed for the fowls. Big round silos of mesh, covered by rooves to keep the main of the water out, now held thousands of maize cobs and really looked very businesslike and promising, if the pigs and sparrows (and rats) left it alone.

Sparrows? Well, if the worst came to the worst, they could and would cover the mesh with netting – "we'll see" they said. Rats could be poisoned if necessary. But pigs? What did you do with hordes of the blessed things, making a mess all about, and ripping out cobs willy-nilly from wherever was convenient. Pulling out six from here, ten from there, three from yonder, and seven more just nextdoor.

John threw up his hands in horror. "They're going to do us in the _____ mongrels. Look! And there! Can you catch them Reg?"

"I can try mate. And yeah! I reckon I can catch some. There's certainly a few around."

All about the cob-cages were hoof-prints of every size, big, small, and bigger. Fresh, older, and five minutes ago it looked like.

"Can I come with you?" Ryan was looking expectantly at his dad and hopefully at me intermittently, face aglow with suppressed fervour.

I hadn't the heart to turn him down and said "Come on then, we'll have a scout around and see what's what."

"How long'll you be Reg?"

"Dunno John, a couple of hours maybe, if we don't get lucky right off. They may have climbed and gone well up or away to bed down, won't know till we start. Why?"

"It's just that we've got to head away a bit earlier today. Should be gone by about four I hope."

Looking at my watch told me we had roughly an hour and three quarters to scare the pigs away and bring at least one home for them to take south.

"C'mon then Ryan. Lets go walkabout. You got a raincoat?"

"Nah."

"Me either. Might get wet soon though. You tough like me?"

"Yep!"

I grinned. Him too, even bigger than me.

"Great then, we're off."

Rebel and co fossicked about a good five minutes and then began to scout about further afield.

Ryan and I climbed slowly in the wake of the dogs. They were seemingly following where the pigs had gone, for all sorts of tracks were seen in the trail we were ascending. But there were other trails too, all covered in hoof marks, all going every-which-where. We could only hope and keep our fingers crossed.

Then as we veered left and entered more thickly grown gorse, the drizzle arrived. It wasn't enough to deter us too much, but as time went on and we climbed higher and higher, it became heavier and the scrub got wetter – and so did we. Ryan never complained a bit. I wanted to, but remembered my comments about being tough and had to "tough it out."

Well above Wes' house now, we turned for home. Or downhill directly towards the road. A flurry of barking had us dashing downwards to where a trickle of water wound its way between hakea trunks and headed where we were going. Shiney's voice petered out as we were half-way down and was heard no more. Thoroughly wet now and feeling just a tad uncomfortable we blundered on down and came out on the road where John and Toni were waiting in their car. Anxious to get away, they had been waiting and heard the dog bark and motored along to beneath the action and there we were, coming out of the scrub like two drowned turkeys, arms hanging out and looking pretty bedraggled. They offered to run me back to my truck but I said "no", I'd be okay.

"I'm pretty tough you know, eh Ryan?"

"Sure am, me too eh!"

So while I was saying goodbye to the Robertsons, Ryan stripped off to his undies and hopped in and out of the rain.

"I'll try again next weekend for you John, maybe sooner – depends. They won't be too far away up the other side – we were just unlucky coming this way."

"Thanks Reg. See you then."

Off they went and I shuffled the half kilometre to my yellow truck and did what Ryan had done.

Once inside and with dry clothes on I felt good again, and only had to hop out as Shiney and Buddy arrived soon after. I'd only just locked them in the box when I saw Tahi coming down from the maize stacks, so got out again to put him away. And no sooner back in the cab than I saw Rebel tracking me along the road, so started up and went to meet him.

A week later we were back again same place, same truck, same dogs, same problem. And more than likely same pigs. It was beautifully fine and sunny, and I was confident of a successful outcome for the dogs had immediately scampered around the maize cribs with noses to the ground and shot off uphill!

I waited in the sunshine listening expectantly. High above Mt. Knobby rose, almost touching the sun it seemed, and clad in dark greens of all sorts, bespeaking heavy manuka and towai forest.

The creek that flowed downwards just below was a good-sized water-course with its head-waters half a kilometre higher up. I knew of a spring under the brow of the highest face that ran all year round and was used by resident swine as a watering-hole in the summer. A couple of wallows a few metres below the spring-head I often visited in the drier hotter weather, and once I recalled, saw a good boar gallop right underneath the large kanuka I was perched in, listening for my dogs. The rifle was on the ground and I only had time to hear his puffing, some heavy footfalls approaching and he shot by, directly beneath me. A black father pig of around 130lb had out-manouvered the dogs and was never heard of

A 122lb pig from behind Maungataraire.

again that day.

Now, as I waited, I didn't anticipate having to climb very far. The dogs were fresh, the wind coming towards us, and anything found now would have to work really hard to gain height and out-distance the hunters.

Then before I was fully awake to it, it was all on, and only 20 metres away . . . Rebel had tracked one down and was scaring the daylights out of a scoffing pig just uphill How the others, even Rebel himself, had missed it initially I don't know. It was almost here. Perhaps it had been coming down anyway. Who knows?

All Rebel knew was that it was the enemy and he set about annoying it immensely. A few more scoffs, some scampering about, a crash, a thud, one yip from my brown dog and they were here. A black boar of around 100lb burst down the small bank and shot between two of the maize stacks. Rebel scragged it momentarily as it swept past me, and it turned on him squealing. In I leapt to grab it's tail, but its snout was where I thought the other end was, and I hastily pulled my hand away and jumped back. Rebel shot at it again and pushed the boar around the other side. Backing up and doing short jabbing runs at the the dog, the two of them danced all around, in and out, backwards and forwards, up and around and down again. I was following, jumping sideways and darting in and away as opportunity and danger presented. Till finally the thing let out a really decent squeal and sat on it's bum. It had had enough of Rebel's ministrations to it's rear end, and I managed to grab it's back leg, then it's tail, as it stood ready to shoot away again. It was it's last chance to get away, for luck had run out for the maize thief. I ended it's depredations beside the maize stack where it had so often gorged itself.

I gutted it on the spot, pleased to have clobbered a good-sized pig for John and Toni, and then put it in the shade of a big gorse plant and waited.

Rebel went sauntering uphill again shortly after and disappeared towards the right and probably crossed the creek. I never heard of him for another half-hour after that, so settled down to await further developments.

But after ten minutes I got restless and began heading into the kanuka, climbing where Tahi and co. had gone.

And then quite suddenly it started again. Above me a short way there was an eruption of snarling and scoffing. I ran a few metres, (it was fairly open) and saw up ahead perhaps another thirty or forty metres, Shiney nutting-off and dancing around a copse of wait-a-while and gahnia. Tahi and Bud were there too going berserk, but beyond, and I couldn't see them. From within came chomping and that boar stench wafted down to envelop me where I stood. Tahi appeared on the left of the thicket, facing inwards and barking non-stop. What a racket!

I inched forward. Something black moved in the gahnia. My rifle came up, but I paused. Where was Buddy? I could hear him just beyond the thicket but daren't shoot. Seconds ticked by and I crept another metre upwards Quietly! Quietly!

The wait-a-while shook and Buddy screamed. Out and in the boar had shot. Leaping back Buddy narrowly avoided being gored – but thought he had been. Shiney and Tahi had leapt in and out too, not yet confident of bettering the big fellow in a punch-up. Again I saw black. The thicket shook and heaved, and out he came like a rocket. A "whoosh", a pounding of hooves, a scattering of dogs, and he was gone, left and up. Never a chance of a shot either. Shiney and Tahi scarpered after him and with Buddy a few metres behind, climbed away and were swallowed by the scrub in seconds.

I heard them a few seconds longer but eventually all was silent. The western front remained all quiet and no more was heard of the big boar for some months.

Disappointed I'd missed the big one, I was still pretty chuffed with Rebel's 100 pounder lying under the gorse bush.

I guessed I'd not hear of the three younger dogs a while yet and got set to head back. Only I hadn't gone ten metres when Rebel opened up again. Half-way up the creek he was bailing good-oh, steady, regular, loud and clear. He sounded as though he was right in the gutter and distant perhaps 150 metres away. Shouldering the rifle freed my hands to ward off shrubbery as I bush-bashed my way towards my number one dog.

I was panting in pretty short measure but clawed away non-stop, trying to get to Rebel before his pig got away. But he seemed to be containing it okay. His barking was pretty consistent and stationary, indicating a pig happy in his position, or more correctly, scared to move out of it.

As I got nearer I slowed down and tried to be still more quiet, but didn't fool Mr. Pig. Coming around a small knoll about fifteen metres distant, but level with the bail, there was another boar looking directly at me. He had heard my approach and was sizing me up, ready to dart off or charge – depending.

But Rebel was on his escape route and still barking pretty consistently. Above him the boar had a rock face that was too high to jump up, with water trickling down. Where he stood glaring at me and the dog, was a slab of rock just big enough for him to stand on, and between him and me was another metre high clay bank. Really, his only way was past Rebel.

I moved slowly closer, wondering how to bring the confrontation to a conclusion. The boar, another of about 100lb, decided for me right then. With a "scoff" he rushed at Rebel, set to speed off. The dog didn't co-operate though. A jig sideways and back as the boar flashed by gave him a mouthful of ear, enough to swing the pig uphill, and enough for me to leap down to grab it's tail.

The knife came out and went in, Mr. Pig shuddered and lay down without another sound, and Rebel let go all about the same time.

Tahi came just then too, all razzed-up and grabbed the comatose pig to savage it a second or two till he realised it was too late and let go He grinned at me as he does and I gave him a pat, Rebel too when he came over. He particularly had done very well and I was thrilled at his performance on this one – as I usually was.

Back at the truck now. I loaded both 100 pounders and opened the dog-box for Rebel and Tahi. Another quarter-hour saw Bud and Shiney turn up and hop in as well, and I went away confident the corn-on-the-cob would have a reprieve a short while now, and John and Toni would be pleased.

(Top dogs find, stop & carry)

'On Yer Bike'

Each year the track gets more overgrown. And each year I tell myself that I really must bring my machete next trip and open it up again. This ritual is gone through in about three year cycles. Year one and it's good, year two it's not so good, and year three it's pretty terrible and the machete comes out.

This year is year three and machete time is tomorrow at 8am.

Kalvin rang last night and wants to bring his dad's mate with him. I had invited him to come and see some new country, a change of scenery for him and his dogs. He jumped at the offer too. They would come in Paul Somers' ute and see me about seven in the morning.

The red sky last night promised a fine day for Saturday which would be great. Where we were going was very tight regrowth gorse and it's pretty horrible trying to get through that stuff when it's wet.

But Saturday brought a lovely day as indeed I had guessed would be the case. It also brought Paul Somers with a dog which was learning the ropes as they say. Kalvin came too, bringing a couple of dogs with him, a couple of pretty experienced dogs actually, and we were fairly confident of coming home with some sort of animal to butcher. That it would be a pig was by no means certain, possums and elephants being quite a possibility, tigers were in with an outside chance – very outside. There could be one escaped from a circus, or zoo, the authorities keeping it all hush-hush so as to not panic the public. And if such a thing happened, and they weren't telling, how would we know? But we weren't too worried. And if we caught an elephant admittedly we'd be surprised, even flabbergasted, but pleased too. Elephants you see, do escape from circuses from time to time – just think of the reward! We hadn't been listening to the radio lately and so didn't know if elephants were on the loose or not – but it was possible – vaguely!

We parked at the usual spot and let the dogs out to get acquainted, donning knife-belts and all the paraphernalia pertaining to hunting. I checked the laces on my rugby boots, my bullets, my knife edge, quantity of string etc etc, and finally declared myself ready to go. Paul and Kalvin had got a little impatient I guess with all my fussing around, and had headed down the track a wee way. But they weren't in a hurry because Kalvin's dogs had got keen under a minute from leaving the vehicles. Just inside the forest edge, only twenty metres from our trucks, and right at the gate, the wild pigs had been at work. Very fresh rooting and digging, not to mention ploughing was evident right at the front gate and Kalvin's dogs had gone "bananas" and disappeared. Mine arrived on the scene probably a minute later and vanished too, into the very tall pines bordering the forest.

We all stood pretty still, ears strained to catch evidence of a chase in progress, a bail-up or a battle going on. But we waited this time in vain. No bark came, or scream from some unlucky pig. One of my younger dogs came back fairly soon, the others staying away hunting another five minutes. Rebel and Tahi prolonged their search but eventually returned as non-plussed as we were as to where the pigs had got to. There was a lot of cover as well, in three and four directions provided by pine trees and gums and endless gorse. They could easily be anywhere and remain unfound even should we hunt all day. A narrow creek meandered along not far below us and beyond this on our right was new country for me. I had explored the land out in front and beyond fairly extensively, with reasonable success in past excursions on this side of the mountain and more recently to a lesser extent down along the creek So where the pigs had got to, while unknown exactly to me was really no great mystery. Somewhere in all that hinterland they were no doubt cosy enough, bedded down among some fern somewhere with trotters crossed in the hopes they'd remain undetected another day or ten.

All seven dogs had returned in the time we waited not far from the forest gate, so then carried on down the dirt track. Rooting was fairly extensive all along here showing of various size pigs having enjoyed themselves during the dark hours. Hoof-prints too told their tale, medium-sized pigs were most common, with the marks of at least one good boar. No tiny sucker-prints were seen and in a way I was glad. No-one wanted to catch baby pigs – what's the point?

Where the track came out of the pines onto a low paddock, Storm suddenly bolted for the swamp. A couple of Muscovy ducks rose shrieking into the air and beat a hasty retreat, disappearing round the bend in the creek but coming back later in a big circle to screech at us as they flew by. Storm was gone by then and we crossed the creek, not in a hurry because really, we were waiting for Storm to turn up, or better still, bark somewhere way ahead of us in the gorse. He didn't though and we never saw him again all day, or until, not long before dark, he arrived trotting up the track looking just as fresh as when he had left us seven hours before.

So on we went, macheteing as we ascended gradually to a forest road. The time spent with the bush-knife was not wasted and while slow enough, provided the dogs ample opportunity to cover the adjoining territory. Pig-runs crossed in numerous places, always with reasonably fresh sign on them and hopes were high. Cobwebs and prickles adorned all three of us fairly extensively, but more so myself being in front. As the track turned left and right through the gorse it was sometimes hard to figure out just where the gap was. After being away all summer, I found the stems and fronds of shrubbery had in many places drooped considerably and sometimes presented quite an obstacle to get through.

Rebel and co. seemed to recognise it straightaway and were at home from the start, checking out each tunnel and gap with zest and enthusiasm. Pig-scent apparently was everywhere and our hunters were having fun yet a hard time sussing out the very freshest and most exciting.

As we stepped out onto the forest road, a change in the intensity of the breeze brought noises from above us. The toi-toi heads rattled slightly, the taller gorse nodded and waved and away at the boundary fence, gum-trees began to move gracefully back and forth.

Kalvin thought he heard a dog bark and shushed me as I started to say something. I heard it too and sucked in my breath. As I glanced at Paul he nodded and pointed ahead. Very thick undergrowth choked a gully that descended in twists and turns from a stand of gum-trees a half-kilometre south. And somewhere up there a dog barked again. A likely place for a boar to hole-up it seemed from where we stood. Let's hope the finder can stay with it a while. The rest of the pack were undoubtedly well on their way – no they weren't. All were seen just then, as we rounded a corner, fossicking about at the culvert. All that is except Storm, who was last seen heading in almost the opposite direction quite some time ago. Kalvin was frowning now and as I asked the question, shook his head slowly.

"I don't think it's Storm Reg. He sounds different to that I reckon.

Could be some other hunter eh?"

"Well, yeah, could be. Do you want to wait for him now then?"

"Nah. He'll come when he's ready. Let carry on".

The breeze was definitely picking up, even if just a little... a cloud cast it's shadow and it seemed cooler somehow. I turned and set off up the road, away from the dog still barking spasmodically up at the head of the gully. I didn't really want to clobber someone else's pig and secretly wished the pig a load of luck.

Concentrating now on the low wide valley on our left, I wondered whether it would be worthwhile heading down the track on the lower side of the road that I knew was just ahead. Or maybe leave it and do the bigger circle. But it had been a while since I had checked out the overgrown track and probably it would be pretty well impassable so may even have to go to plan C and keep on the road.

The dogs decided for us. Coming to the landing road half way up the hill Rebel and Tahi scarpered left, looking pretty lively and weren't seen again inside a quarter-hour. Kalvin's other dog followed, Shiney too, and only Bud remained to guard us mere mortals.

Rebel opened up a good way off in the mid-age pines. In the direction he and Tahi had gone and slightly downhill, his voice came authoritatively "Stop and wait – or else." But the pig didn't stop, thumbing it's nose so to speak, at my main dog and putting one trotter after another at speed, headed for another place.

Rebel stuck with him though, mean dog that he was, and tormented the daylights out of him at every opportunity. We were running now, down the landing road-come overgrown track and pulled up at the discarded logs and butts at the end. We'd heard Tahi once on our dash down but were apprehensive now as we stopped, as no fresh indication of the chase had come our way the last couple of minutes. Had they lost it?

We leapt ahead a second later as a heavy squeal rang out not 100 metres away, between us and the side-creek. Trouble was, navigating the piled-up trash and left-over logs was slow going and leadership changed several times as Kalvin, Paul and I tried to find a way through and around. Tall old-man gorse was main cover beyond though and not really too hard to slither and crash between or around, and in no time we were dispatching a 70lb black boar whose luck had ran out. All the dogs were there at the kill except Kalvin's Storm, and most participated in the free feed that ensued. Bud was engrossed in downing the heart and

Tahi was half way though his allocation of liver when Rebel and Shiney took off in a great hurry downstream. Bud and Tahi caught on too and belted after where Kalvin's dog had also gone. Seconds passed, and then an almighty fracas erupted only fifty metres away. Dropping what we were doing, we darted between the gorse-trunks, me with the rifle in my fist, going to lend a hand. Caution dictated our approach for we knew it was a boar. The pong assailing our nostrils told us a large male wild pig was being beset by the pack of dogs and we slowed somewhat. As we came upon the scene of the battle it was obvious our bailers were again forgetful of their proper roles and were holding, or attempting to hold a 120lb boar who was pretty riled up. He tossed them about and moved approximately five or six metres further back even as we watched. The lighter dogs were certainly in with a will but would have benefited with the few more kilos of bodyweight had they been born-and-bred holders. Nevertheless, it was one of those easier approaches you are dealt occasionally and I snuck in, grabbed the big bushy tail and delivered the "coup-de-grace".

Kalvin's dog had been right there along with mine and we grinned like a trio of schoolboys as we slapped each other on the back or the shoulder. What could be better then this eh? Good weather, good dogs, good company and good pigs. Yeah! – we were pretty stoked, and spent a considerable time chewing the fat – and still grinning.

Those grins faded after a while though as we began to contemplate hefting the two carcasses out to a vehicle, or somewhere we could get one to.

I looked at Kalvin, then looked at the two pigs, and back and Kalvin. How do you do this?

"The big pig should go with the biggest joker I reckon," I said dead pan, "and the lighter one with the smaller chap. Stand up Kalvin, and let's see who's the biggest most muscular, tough, rugged and formidable out of the two of us."

He stood slowly with a frown on his face, which soon gave way to a whimsical grin again.

"You win, I lose," he said graciously (I knew all the time).

It was a bit of a battle getting back to the road with our respective burdens afterwards. We had backtracked to the jumble of logs and butts at the landing. Smashing and breaking gorse stems on the way there and back to make a track of sorts. Particular attention was paid to branches and drooping fronds at head height and just above. This was done to facilitate carrying the pigs out "piggy-back" when their snouts, protruding above our heads, would otherwise catch on the same. If it wasn't done they would undoubtedly become b___ branches and f__ __ fronds (blimmin' branches and flippin' fronds). These were to be avoided at all costs and the effort and time put into dealing to them beforehand was considered well spent.

The bigger boar, being the last caught, was where our newly cut track started from. We had yet to return to the the seventy pounder (if we could find it) and finish tying it up preparatory to carrying it out before we could follow in Kalvin's wake.

Back now at the aforesaid bigger boar, we loaded it onto Kalvin's broad back and sent him on his way. Calling back over his shoulder he asked: "You sure you can find your pig Reg?"

"Yeah, I reckon, it's only about fifty or sixty metres over there, we'll be right."

And by the time we did find it and start the hard stuff, Kalvin was well out of sight and sound. I hurried through the tying up process and struggled to my feet, Paul having to carry the rifle now and break trail. When doing so for someone else who is doing the carrying behind me, I pay particular attention to twigs and branches around head-height, these being the ones the pig's snout invariably gets tangled in. When carrying myself, as now, the going is quite a lot slower – and even more so if carrying a freshly killed animal. After a half-hour or so the pig's head and neck will have stiffened up due to rigor-mortis and sit more firmly on the shoulders, whereas a newly killed and gutted animal will literally flop all over the place, first one side, then the other, and catch on every conceivable piece of greenery available.

I reckoned Kalvin would have had quite a battle with the bigger pig as he was on his way only fifteen minutes after it was killed. Until he emerged onto the landing road, that flopping head would have been a real headache to him. Mine wasn't really much better, though some, and I eventually made it to find Kalvin well gone. The "sort-of-track" was now fairly well overgrown with gorse and cutty-grass howbeit with a semi-smashed-down walkway, or struggle-way back up to the metalled road. I attacked it at an even pace, one foot after another and keeping my mind carefully blank (wouldn't be hard Robbie Elliot reckons) just persevered to the junction. I could turn now uphill, Yay! Way to go!

About his time Paul decided his hip was telling him to call it a day

Paul Somers and author at the jumble of logs and butts.

and reckoned he'd head on back to his truck and wait for us at the gate along the road. He was due for a hip replacement operation which wasn't too far off, so thought it wise to not aggravate his condition much more today. It worked out pretty good in the end as it meant our two boars didn't have to be carried back through that head-high gorse.

As Paul turned and hobbled back down the hill, I turned and started up the hill again. And there about a hundred metres distant was Kalvin lying down on the roadside, his pig lying beside him, his arms outstretched as he lay on his back. Recovery time! I wasn't sure whether he was having a blow, or having a spell, but on pulling up alongside decided it was a spell! His blowing had subsided five minutes back, and he was now simply recuperating.

"Good idea mate," I said as I shucked off my pig too, and flopped down in the shade beside him. It's a wonderful feeling that, with the weight gone, you feel as though you could fly, being light-shouldered those first few seconds (light-headed for me – Robbie Elliot again).

I think I must have dozed off for Kalvin's cough some time later had me come-to with quite a start.

"Any pig lice on your's Reg? Mine's pretty lousy. I'm thinking of cutting both their heads off."

"Go for it Kal. Don't forget to bury the bodies. Conservation –

101

environment contamination. You know!"

"Aw, shucks."

"Aw shucks nothing. With seventy-five less lice to carry you may – just may, be able to keep up with me though."

I got to me feet and climbed into my burden again. Kalvin just lay there with his eyes tight shut.

"You want a hand Kal?"

"No, No mate. I'll be all right. You go on ahead. I'll catch up in a minute or two, it's not too heavy."

With that assurance reverberating around inside my head – (it's all right Elliot, I know what your thinking) I set off again, this time though, still climbing slightly and I entered a stand of mature pines where the tops closed in and kept the road in shade all day. Being refreshed and in the shade, I was able to walk along at a good pace and came eventually to another junction. Here I turned left, and walking partly in shade and partly in sun, kept going another two kilometres, the road dipping and rising but keeping mostly on the ridge-top.

A long time later I rounded the last corner, all four of my dogs still trotting beside me and saw at the gate, Paul's Hilux, at the end of the journey. How thankful I was to be able to dump my load! And rub my sore shoulders ! And sit down as Paul offered me an orange.

"Where's Kalvin Reg? He got lost or something?" Paul was inspecting my pig as he asked the obvious and all I could say was something like "He's coming with the bigger boar, soon."

"Yeah, right!"

"What? What do you mean?"

"Have a look," said Paul, shaking his head.

And there, only 100 metres behind me all the way had been my mate – minus his boar, he must have had a real struggle keeping up, what with the sun overhead much of the way and me pushing it with my load to get to the gate before dark. Poor beggar was a bit wobbly-kneed when he pulled up, and red in the face too – honest."

I looked at him frowning, looked at Paul trying not to laugh and finally said, trying to frown again but not quite succeeding.

"Yeah, right!"

"No, truly -"

"Where did you leave it?"

"Where I was when you took off. I was going to follow you straight away but couldn't get the confounded thing off the ground. It must be at least 150lb. I'm sorry Reg." Kalvin seemed genuinely concerned he had let me down and I didn't have the heart to berate him over-much.

"It's okay mate, not to worry. It would have been a fair haul for you if you had've made it. Don't worry, we'll go home and have a feed and come back in the dark."

Paul took us back to where we had stashed my ute and Kalvin's van. And declining a "cuppa" back at my place, headed immediately for Kaitaia and home. Kalvin was feeling bad about his aborted attempt at carrying the trophy pig of the day and not saying much, apart form offering to go back and have another go after tea. I wasn't saying much either and was feeling a bit tired after the day's outing, so just sat eating my tea and thinking hard. A plan was formulating in my mind, a clever cunning plan, and after a while I started to smile just a wee bit. I was starting to feel good and even relaxed and recounted for Olive the day's hunt. What we'd heard, where we'd run, the size of our boar, who killed it, and so on. She's always been a good listener and I got lot of enjoyment out of retelling the whole thing. Even needling Kalvin a little too was fun – for me. Kalvin and I ate, not hurriedly, but kept an eye on the clock, thinking of the next stage of the exercise and the possibility of the midnight gong sounding ere we'd finished.

It was well dark by the time we had done eating and we went outside to put a big wad of string on my truck, toss on my ten-speed push-bike and speed away in clean, dry clothes. Kalvin brought his van as well as he needed to get to bed before at least 5am. His alarm was set to go at six, and he would have to get some shut-eye!

The moon was pretty well full and gave good lighting as we set off along the forest road. Me biking with a Big-Jim lantern in one hand and Kalvin walking, intending to meet me on my return and lend a bit of muscle for the uphills. With no permit (it had run-out) I still wasn't too concerned. Likely there would be no-one out and about at this hour except maybe other fly-by-nighters. And probably they'd slink away successfully, even if I failed.

The boar was just where I'd last seen it some hours before, two kilometres in and still tied ready to carry. Getting it untied and stretched out, what with rigor-mortis to contend with and loaded and tied on my bike in the dark all by myself was quite some chore. I went fifty metres and found it wasn't far enough forward, it's bum acting as a brake on the rear tyre. By this time I was under the tall pines again and in some pretty deep gloom. I couldn't sit my torch anywhere that would allow

The 137 pounder on the bike.

it to shine on my ropes, and it was too big to hold in my teeth so had to resort to feel and guess work, but eventually got it sorted and set off again. Going downhill and along level ground was no sweat, but the jolly hills weren't as jolly as they had been on the way in. But Kalvin had exceeded himself and done remarkably well, meeting me much sooner than I had anticipated, and for this I was profoundly thankful. With him on the other side, and talking good-oh again, the time in the moonlight among the pines, illegally and clandestinely (definitely not poaching) was in the end really quite enjoyable. We caught several more bigger, cantankerous and stroppy boars on the way (with the help of the shadows and stillness of the night) but thankfully didn't have to carry these out. We "made-do" with the 137 pounder on the bike and made the gate around 11pm. It was a first for NZ I thought – but have seen pictures of, and heard of other boars on bikes since. I seem to remember something about a parade once down Queen St in Auckland made up of boars on bikes, or some such. Come to think of it, it was motor bikes and – and something beginning with B anyway.

Kalvin Comes Through

Kalvin rang one mid-summer Friday night, wanting to know if I was keen for a run behind the dogs the following day. He knew where we'd likely get a run he reckoned and was all fired up. A young friend, name of Roland was going to tag along too, as well as a new dog he had called Bruce, given him by a mate.

Unfortunately I had a prior engagement and couldn't make it, even though I'd have loved to go walkabout with him. His dogs were performing exceptionally well and more than likely, if they did find one, would actually pull it up. I was tempted to have a lapse of memory as regards that engagement jacked up before he rang, but did the proper thing and told him to go bush without me. This is what he told me had happened.

Roland was still as keen as mustard, as only a sixteen-year-old can be, all optimism and positive thinking, utterly convinced of success – even if they failed. That they would catch a big boar was written in the wind, as sure as eggs and that God made little apples (yeah, sure He did – and big ones too). He was actually quite excited and had it all mapped out in his mind. A huge black tusker was a "cert."

The wind (in which supposedly it was written) dropped a mite late in the afternoon and Roland suddenly became convinced that even if not a big tusker, they would at least catch a boar. The wind died still further and when last Kalvin spoke to him – around 9pm – he was told they'd catch some sort of a pig in the morning, no doubt about it.

At 5am Kalvin called around to Roland's place. It was still dark with not a glimmer in the eastern sky, no moon at all now either, and the air was as still as ever it could be.

"Still reckon we'll get a pig Roland?" Kalvin asked quite innocently.

"Should find one at least."

Kalvin kept quiet another quarter kilometre and heard "– don't you think Kalvin?"

Roland sounded a little less convinced, and with his mate just smiling to himself and glancing sideways at him now and then, came out with – "I've always wanted to hunt Puketi anyway. Even just a walk would be good eh – eh Kalvin?"

"Sure mate, sure."

Turning his head now Roland looked at the dogs in the back of the van and decided that with Blue, Tango, Storm and Bruce out scenting around, their chances of a big black 170 pounder were still reasonably good. Blue, a blue-heeler cross was probably main dog and about in his prime – around four years old and actually doing pretty well of late. If there was a boar to be found, Blue would do the finding all right, of that he was confident. Storm too did a lot of hunting and was no mean stopping-dog himself. This animal was a black and white cattle dog cross something, and only young yet as well. Then of course there were Tango and Bruce to back them up and the more he thought about it as Kalvin drove, the more his optimism kicked in again.

It took an hour or more to get to Puketi and day was just breaking as the two hunters and their dogs disembarked at the pink gates. These were well known among the hunting fraternity – a good place to begin looking, and were at the eastern end, more or less, of the Mokau ridge. A good few kilometres long, Mokau ridge dominated the skyline away back into the heart of the Puketi forest and became part of the whole Puketi/Omahuta upland region of bushclad ridges, huge mist-shrouded valleys, big rivers and frothing streams, and mighty trees left untouched by the loggers of bygone days. Here lived the wild cattle and goats, "captain-cookers" and kiwi, rosellas and kokako and King Tiriana.

I'm not sure if this legendary boar ever was caught, though if he was his mantle and mana would be passed on to some other worthy tusker deep in the confines of the undergrowth. Always there was some notorious, secretive, half alluded to huge rogue boar hidden away in the back of beyond. Hunted and hounded all his life, he became so cunning and elusive that no one knew for sure where he lived. A dog would be killed at one end of the vast forest region and immediately it would be King Tiriana's work. The hunter, even though not having seen this huge pig had heard it crash away and found his other dogs not at all keen to give chase. And a month and a half later the same story would unfold miles away. To Tiriana, or The King as he became known, was attributed the demise of another good pig dog or two and now, the year of our Lord 2006, it wasn't entirely safe or advisable to venture alone anywhere in all that vastly unplotted and unexplored hinterland.

Nothing much had been heard of this supposed king of the forest a good while now. Perhaps he had died, succumbed to old age and passed on. That he had massive tusks went without saying as most of his progeny from this region sported unusually good hooks themselves. If this were true, another King Tiriana would rise to fame in the folklore of hunters who skirted the perimeter; and so the legend lived on.

According to rumour one of the Whittaker boys had caught a very big pig, though with touches of ginger in it last year, and it was assumed it was King Tiriana's heir apparent. A massive boar weighing well over 200lbs, it had "put paid" to one or two dogs before being bettered and dragged out to civilisation. Now it seemed the infamous slayer of hounds had "gone bush" and disappeared into the depths of the forest and remained unheard of for months on end. Possibly he was alive somewhere and lying low, but no-one knew for sure.

Roland and Kalvin walked along the road. They had left their vehicle at the pink gates, and shouldering the rifle, set off to find a poaka. The mid-summer sun beat down and soon had the boys shedding jerseys to wrap around their waists. They still had to carry the weight but at least they wouldn't sweat quite so much.

They rounded a corner with the sun directly behind them now, casting long shadows on the downhill slope in front and both were startled when a pheasant shot into the air crowing, and flapped off over the rise to disappear among the trees. They hadn't seen it in the shadows and came to a sudden halt, long enough to see it was only a bird as it finally glided out of sight.

Starting off again they were aware that even the hunting dogs weren't into their thing yet to any great extent. Blue was most often out in front, but only by fifty metres or so and stayed on the verge practically all the time. It seemed there wasn't much of interest to pig dogs today. The other three, Bruce, Storm and Tango were content to tag along behind, mooching as pooches do.

An hour had gone by and though the boys, had warmed up, the air was still cool enough, while down in the valleys, not seen often through the trees, mist was still clinging in the sheltered basins, and shadows lingered in the lee of higher peaks.

Another hour sped by and nothing much had happened.

The air was warmer, the walk had become a stroll with frequent pauses to gaze away to the horizon, or wonder at the lack of interest

Kalvin with a 104lb boar.

seen in the dogs. Roland's "big boar for sure" was now a piglet of his imagination, and looked like becoming a decided figment the longer the journey became.

Piwakawaka was a constant companion. This little bird favoured the sunny places it seemed as it flittered and fluttered everywhere just beyond reach, gathering tiny insects on the wing. Roland remarked on the fantail and wished the dogs showed as much interest in hunting as piwakawaka did.

"If they put as much energy into finding as those fantails did we'd have one by now Kal."

"Dead right mate," Kalvin agreed. "Plenty of time yet though. Just be patient. We haven't seen much sign yet don't forget. Only that bit back there."

On a landing alongside the road a short way back Kalvin had pointed out the marks of a good pig in a muddy hole. Ghania and gorse had pretty well covered the landing by now and beneath the fronds of the cutty-grass bushes a small puddle had remained, enough to let them see marks of trotters embedded there – but the 100lb pig that had made them had well gone.

The road wound along the ridge-top heading generally west. Tall trees obscured much of the distant view and the gentle ups and downs of their progress were bounded by an untold and uncounted profusion of manuka, gorse, mingi-mingi and kumarahoe. Up on the batters, reindeer-fern, spleenwort and tupake thrived along with mosses and lichen and tiny seedlings of all sorts.

It was rather pleasant to be honest and Kalvin decided to wait a while for at last Blue had disappeared and been gone fifteen minutes. He had ducked under some small ghania bushes on the right-hand side and not been seen since. So this decided the boys/men to kill two birds with one stone and sit in the fern in a sunny spot out of the breeze and wait until something transpired.

"Have you fellows caught pigs around here Kal," Roland asked as he lay back with eyes shut.

"A few, not many. Nothing much any good for more'n twelve months though."

"Mm," was Roland's reply, and a short while later "Zzzz."

Fast asleep, the youngster didn't hear the flight of the kereru as they winged past, the characteristic beat – beat – beat of their wings alerting Kalvin who was still awake and listening for his number one dog to sound. They flew to the right of a stand of kahikatea pines and were gone, though some time later returned and headed back where they came from.

The breeze, coming now out of the west, stirred the seed-heads of some toi-toi at his back and Kalvin was thankful to get even a slight wind coming from where he guessed Blue was. The toi-toi fronds weren't quite ripe but rustled and scraped together desultorily as the puff and huff of the air caught them from time to time.

Nor did Roland hear what Kalvin did twenty minutes later. Barking out towards Omaunu Road. Blue's barking! Once fairly near and twice more a little later further away. He'd been gone now for over forty minutes and Kalvin was just a tad anxious, too alert to have gone to sleep but did have his eyes shut at the moment. Wide awake now he saw Storm, Tango and Bruce hurtle away towards Omaunu Road and Blue's call.

Their scarpering, stones being kicked up and a yip from Bruce hadn't been enough to awaken Roland. Kalvin stood up and moved to the top of the next rise leaving him "stacking zeds".

Blue didn't pull the pig immediately and Kalvin guessed it was not a small one to so out-distance the cunning and fit finder as it seemed to have done. No more noise was heard from Blue though and five minutes went by before the other three dogs returned. They still had ears cocked and stared pointedly north and west to where they reckoned they had heard their kennel-mate sing out.

Kalvin moved on again leaving Roland fast asleep and topped the next rise towards the west. Fortunately the road still ran in that direction more or less and he had gained a little height now. At his back were acres upon acres, falling not too steeply away towards a river a long way off, covered in kahikatea and karaka, rimu and puriri. Taraire were very common among them too; and at various places their heads showing clearly where they towered over all, stood the stately kauri, a monarch among the trees. Dark green above lesser shades, the whole effect immensely peaceful and settling, their tops spoke of aeons of sunshine and rain, wind and calm and days upon days of just being. Nothing seemed to move or change and a hunter felt so infinitesimal and insignificant, the chase of no consequence at all and Kalvin wondered why he was there.

That piwakawaka again! They were still here, and they darted about catching their food as they flew – and seemed somehow to fit, to be part of that whole big picture. Kalvin surmised that even kauri too had to feed and were doing so as he waited, drawing moisture and nutrients from the soil, carbondioxide from the air, growing and reaching higher as even now they dominated all below.

"I've got to eat too you know," he told them, feeling as though in some way he was trespassing, creating a disturbance in this seemingly tranquil scene. His quietly spoken thoughts were mitigation he hoped – one could easily understand folk of long ago asking Tane, god of the forest, for his blessing on their hunt. But Kalvin reckoned that the God who inspired the bible knew all about that for He recorded this – "All the beasts of the forest are mine and the cattle upon a thousand hills," (Psalm 50:10). Then there's this indictment for all those no-hopers who leave good pork in the bush just because they're too lazy to hump it out.

"The lazy man does not roast what he takes when he is hunting,"

(Proverbs 12:27). So apparently it would be okay if Blue stopped that confounded pig he had seen, so he and Roland could carry it out to an oven somewhere!

I'm a bit selfish I suppose when it comes to giving away pork. Olive often does give the stuff away, but she knows now never to give away the shanks, my favourite piece on the whole pig. I guess Kalvin was anticipating something the same as he waited anxiously for Blue to bark again.

Roland came briskly over the rise, his eyebrows raised in question as he took in Kalvin standing in the middle of the road, head tilted sideways and mouth open. He raised his hand as Roland was about to speak, and they both sought to hear a summons from Blue somewhere way out in front.

"There Kal! Hear it?" Roland pointed excitedly to where a small knoll was covered in towai and rewarewa trees. Interspersed were many mahoe and matipo trees, lighter green than the mid-shade of the others but all were much shorter than the larger rimu and taraire on adjoining ridges. Yet it wasn't to the knoll itself that Roland was pointing so vigorously, but rather away beyond, lower down from where a bark – a definite bark, had come.

"Was it Blue d'you think?" This from Kalvin who hadn't heard a thing.

"Heck, a bark's a bark isn't it? I heard it!" Roland was convinced again.

"Why don't you head down there then. I'll hang around a wee bit more – just in case he moves again. Meet you back here later on." Kalvin had glanced at the dogs who apparently hadn't heard the bark claimed so enthusiastically by his young friend. If Blue had barked so clearly as Roland claimed, why hadn't Tango, Bruce and Storm already gone? It was rather incongruous in the light of Roland's adamant claim, so Kalvin decided to cover both bases. Allowing Roland to hive off on his own into a large unfamiliar bush wasn't as silly as it might seem. He had been on a good number of other hunts and had shown himself pretty level-headed and would have no trouble climbing back to the road running right along the main ridge. Besides, Kalvin wasn't too convinced. He himself had last heard his main dog further along and wanted to be on hand in case he barked subsequently, and were he in the bush with Roland on a wild pig chase, not hear.

Storm suddenly stormed off along the road, and there at his shoulder was young Bruce, flat out for the horizon. (This was only 100 metres in front). Kalvin and Tango heard it then too and were off as well, following Bruce and Storm along the road. Probably it was what Roland had heard, but having misplaced it's source, had gone off at a tangent.

Not to worry. Again Blue sounded, still a fair way off but seeming to come from down another ridge that Kalvin was fast approaching.

He turned right, ducked the low branches of a mahoe tree and bustled along at his best clip towards the action. Ten minutes had gone since he first heard it and he was now well down the fairly open ridge. But as he came to an abrupt drop-off he heard the pig squeal, down below still and almost on the lower part of the ridge. Blue had come through for him, as he usually did and he confidently clambered lower using his hands just here and entered thick, more tangled understorey. Disappointed at the squeal he heard, he was never-the-less relieved he'd found Blue and seen the other dogs go in support. Teamwork it was. He and Roland were a team as well, had split up to ensure one or the other found the kill.

A few more metres to go. Suddenly he realised the little squealer was moving uphill towards him , albeit slowly as three very tenacious dogs hampered his progress. That human smell, known to this boar from way back had further enraged him and he decided to take out the man if possible first. Kalvin hesitated. What to do? Bruce was barking continuously and Kalvin was hoping Roland would arrive – but not counting on it. They were a fair way from where he had headed, and it would all be across country for him, so he got behind a larger tree and waited. Sure enough the boar turned sideways and showed his immense shoulder and flank. This was no mean weaner – no way! He looked more like a 150 pounder, and those hooks! Wow!

"I'd better get in and help the dogs", he thought. All three bailers were holders now that the boss had arrived. But they weren't over-heavy holders and looked to Kalvin for support as they hung on. Just at the right second he dove in, grabbed a back leg and slipped his blade between the boar's ribs. It was over. The old battler took a short while to realise he was dead but sank slowly, tiredly down and rested his chin on the ground. Those enormous tusks, so deadly moments ago, but now in repose, stuck up and out eye-catchingly as they lay in front of their grinders. The tips, remarkably thin and razor-sharp were ivory-white, deadly daggers that Kalvin would come to treasure more and more, even as he now admired them. A set like these were not often come by and he was over the moon that he now had a jaw to compare well with any.

He couldn't afford to sit and enjoy the moment too long in case Roland passed by on the road way above. Setting to, he gutted the prize and putting it over his shoulder (he guessed it wouldn't after all go 150lb), began the long, slow, laborious haul up and out.

It took fifteen minutes just to get it up to the top of the drop-off, then after a blow another twenty minutes hard slog to the road. Here he shucked it off just inside the scrub and floated the last four metres to stand in the sunshine and await his mate.

The walkie-talkie spluttered and squawked a second later and Kalvin reached for his set to answer queries he knew Roland would have.

"You got one Kal?"

"Yeah, just a weaner. You?"

"Nah, couldn't hear much really."

"Where are you now then?"

"On the road where I started. Where are you?"

"On the road too. About three small rises further along. It's only about five minutes walking. Come and give us a hand!"

"You won't need –." Kalvin had shut the thing off on purpose and a few minutes later Roland turned up.

"Where's your weaner?"

"Oh, just in the shade there," Kalvin replied nonchalantly. "Stick it on your back and we'll get started back."

Roland sauntered over. He could see the blood on Kalvin's shirt so knew he wasn't kidding and was all set to heave a fifty/sixty pounder over his shoulder and begin the long march.

"Great jumping Jehosaphat!" Roland's exclamation and consternation seemed peculiarly funny to Kalvin and he burst out laughing. Roland knew he had been had but wasn't peeved at all. Truly he was pleased for Kalvin, for them both. Hadn't he been in on the hunt! Hadn't he heard it first! Lucky he'd alerted Kalvin eh! Wouldn't they have something to brag to Reg about and nag him over. "Prior commitments" – what a laugh. He could have his "prior commitments". Couldn't compare with this – "Eh Kal."

Kalvin was pretty pleased himself and helped get the boar on Roland's back and set sail for the van some two and a half hours steady walking away. They had turns and carried it to where it got to be 200 pounds and chucked it off – time for a change. In the mid-day sun it needed the other to drive the carrier on with words of encouragement and praise.

"Useless young punk! Can't even go uphill. When I was your age I

Kalvin with a 165lb barrow, Takahue.

carried one and a half times that size for Dad. You must be soft." Kalvin did his best to put a bit of steel in Roland's spine for him. But youngkers are youngkers and it befell Kalvin to do the carrying again. Another half hour spell would have them almost to the pink gates. Roland was pretty quiet. He was saving his breath – he wasn't quite sure whether his so-called mate was needling him to more effort or was genuinely disgusted with his effort. He kept his own counsel and hefted the boar for the last ten minute's almost flat walk. Kalvin was behind a little way now as Roland stepped along, trying to keep Blue at heel. An up-draught from the north where a ferny face showed had brought something alluring to the dogs again and Blue in particular was keen to go.

"Heel Blue," Kalvin repeated several times. "Heel Storm, heel!"

A few moments later, still keeping an eye on Storm and Blue and Co, Kalvin caught up again just as Roland dumped the pig at the pink gates.

"Good on you mate. You've done really well. You'll make a hunter yet I reckon." Kalvin was now lavish in his praise and young Roland beamed. Coming from Kalvin, this was praise indeed and he smiled and smiled – and stopped smiling the next moment.

"Kalvin!"

"What's up?" Roland was staring at the wheels of their vehicle.

114

"Look!"

He did, and let out a groan. Some low-down, low-life had slashed all four tyres. No one owned the pink gates, or the country out beyond. It was pure nastiness done out of jealousy no doubt. Stupid, uncalled for small-mindedness and meanness had instilled in someone's no-brain the thought to perform this act of callousness and cowardice. They could have left a note of some sort, waited to argue or fight over what wasn't their's anyway, but resorted instead to being petty and disgusting and small.

They walked some distance and were able to borrow wheels from a farmer – there were decent people in the world after all, and being thankful for the help provided, headed for home and a brew. No ripped dogs was a bonus, camaraderie among mates another, and a really good set of hooks helped overcome the disappointment of such a dastardly deed.

"Only a bastard would do that eh Kalvin!"

"You're right there Roland, only a dastardly bastard! But wait till we ring Reg. I'll bet he'll wish he'd come too."

And I WAS disappointed to have missed out, certainly. But them's the pickings. To honour one's word is just as important I reasoned. Yet to catch one of Tiriana's progeny was something else again for sure. Better still to be in on the action when they catch the "King" himself one day. And maybe I'll be there next time Kalvin comes through.

Mates And Memories

Here are some pictures of mates and the type of pigs that make memories:

Peter Greenhill and a pig from Utukura.

Punga, Fluffy and Maunga with Kalvin. The pig was 140lb from Takahu.

Kalvin again this time the pig was 134lb.

Tahi giving a pig swimming lessons.

A good boar with broken tusks, Peter Greenhill's catch.

Above – Peter Greenhill and a 183lb pig from Bartons.
Left – Peter again this time with a 133lb boar getting out from Snake Gully.

Peter's 110lb pig was quite garrulous, Kiwi the dog, was a bit more sceptical.

Paul Ogle with 142lb of pork and a long walk ahead of him..

Peter 's team and a 143lb pig not far from Whangarei.

Guess who? The callous slayer of swine!

"That blasted gorse." Peter Greenhill and team at the Oruaiti River.

Peter and Kiwi at Matawaia with a 110lb of pork.

Did Brett Roycroft ride this one literally into the ground? Good hooks and 118lb.

Des Sand's favourite way to carry a 104lb pig.

Ripped To Smithereens

Because I don't do very much hunting over the summer months the dogs miss out on a lot of practice and tend to become unfit and rather fat. Comes late March and I'm rarin' to go, dogs too, but we're all rather useless in the scrub for a month or two. I've been sitting on a bulldozer all summer and have succumbed to flab rather than muscle; I doubt I'll ever get fat but the muscle-tone and fitness have gone out the window. By end of September we're all as fit as buck rats again, the 'dozer is ready to do long hours and we revert to our summer languor and lassitude in the seat.

Therefore when Kalvin Roycroft rang from Kaitaia and offered to hunt a couple of my dogs for me, I jumped at the chance. He hunted all year round and I reckoned it would do Tahi and Bud good to get some more practice. They would definitely see a few good pigs running with Blue and Spot and co. and this could only be to their advantage, so Kalvin and Brett (his dad) came out and picked up the two young dogs who were going to stay with them for a while.

The following Friday Kalvin rang another friend, an older experienced hunter by the name of Paul Somers.

"Gidday Paul, Kalvin here. What are you up to tomorrow?"

"Not too sure yet Kal. I've got to mow the lawn sometime I know."

"Cor! That can wait can't it? I'm going hunting at Puketi and thought you might like to come too. Bring Mo for a run if you like."

"Well, yeah! I guess it won't hurt to leave it for Monday. What time are you going to get away?"

"I thought about five. That okay with you? We've got over an hour to go to get there and we don't want to be too late. What do you reckon?"

"Sounds good to me Kal. I'll be ready – and thanks." Paul was still awaiting a summons for a knee replacement operation and was grateful for a chance to go on an outing where the walking wasn't all uphill or downhill. The road in the bush would be handable he reckoned and was looking forward to giving his eighteen month old greyhound, bull-cattle cross dog some more action, preferably on a pig or two.

Kalvin arrived bang on time and Mo and Paul were soon stashed inside and they were on their way. The van fair hummed along the highway but slowed down somewhat on the winding corners of the Mangamukas. I've counted the corners both up and down a couple of times but have forgotten now how many there are, enough to keep you awake at any rate. The heavy bush and steep gullies, rugged ridges and cathedral quietness of the place call to any hunter traversing this gorge and so it was today. Even though it wasn't yet daylight, they both knew it well and were lost in thought as they sped south. How many big boars were there hiding in all that labyrinth of forest and bush gullies, ferny faces and big high tops?

Just personally I can waste hours of time simply staring off into the vista ahead, daydreaming, seeing myself and my dogs walking slow and carefree along that far dark green saddle. Which way would I go? The clouds high above me winged fairly swiftly away to the east-south-east, so I'd have to climb that steep-looking but short ridge to where a stand of kauri made the skyline. Probably there'd be --?

But I wasn't even there. Kalvin and Paul motored on south still, past Umawera and Rangiahua and turned off onto Puketi West Road.

"Not far to go now eh Kalvin," Paul stirred and peered ahead. The daylight was coming and soon there'd be things to see. The driver changed down to climb up alongside a valley on the left with vertical walls, over one of which tumbled a high waterfall.

"I'd hate to have a pig get too near that with my dogs hanging on," said Kalvin. "You'd lose the whole flamin' lot for sure."

My brothers-in-law, Andrew and Trevor, had just that happen on the seaward side of the Whangaroa harbour years ago. The boar and three dead dogs at the base of the cliff were what greeted them when they finally arrived. But it wasn't likely here, not where they were going today.

Pulling into his usual spot Kalvin checked to make sure he had his permit with him, locked the van after letting the dogs out and did a couple of stretches. Paul did likewise and bent down to tie boot laces again, hefted the small back-pack he usually took along and began their quest in earnest.

It was lovely to be out and about and the two just sauntered along, giving the dogs plenty of time. Blue and Spot, five and three years old respectively were keen to work and set about immediately inspecting every clump of grass, water-hole, cut-out, ghania bush and tree-trunk. Storm, only a younker yet of about eighteen months had had a few pigs and quickly got the idea to follow the two older dogs back and forth. My two, Bud and Tahi, at five and four years old knew what pigs were too but hadn't had the experience that Kalvin's older dogs had, but even they, Paul's dog Mo included, seemed like pig dogs today and did their share of pretending to scent for pig-sign. Mine were bailing type dogs whereas Paul's and Kalvin's were more inclined to hold where they could, each one having a bit of mastiff or bulldog/bull-terrier in their make-up somewhere. If a big boar was pulled up it would be advisable to get there pronto as the number of dogs present would tend to give them all a bit of "Dutch-courage" and they'd more than likely sail in too early and get towelled-up.

After an hour's walking they came to where Kalvin and I caught two big billy-goats a year previous. I think it was Rebel and Tahi who had been at fault and we had managed to let one go and shoot the other, and deal with the offending parties.

Today, not wanting a repeat of last time, Kalvin opted to go left and down another track just before getting to our goat country. Here a small weaner was caught and released and the party changed tracks again, electing to stay on higher ground heading roughly eastwards. More and more kauri were seen and less gorse grew along the roadside – surely a good omen?

But tute was plentiful hereabouts and just now drooped with heaps of small flower-like clusters of seed-heads. White butterflies were in profusion; whatever they were after was a mystery. I always thought of them as cabbage-eaters and of course there were no cabbages around here. They fluttered all over the place – perhaps they were on migration somewhere – but certainly kept the scene alive with their seemingly haphazard dodging and fluttering about. Many birds too were a-wing today and the sunshine definitely told of summer and heat and long days.

The men ambled along, content to bide their time. It was early days yet at 10am. And the dogs just now were picking up a scent from somewhere ahead it seemed. Kalvin was quite adept at reading Blue's actions and guessed whatever it was that sent that tantalising scent on the breeze was as yet some distance away. Spot was looking decidedly business-like at the same time and followed where Blue trotted with

A good one of Buddy and Storm.

head up and nose in overdrive. Something was in the wind!

Just ahead the country dropped off quite steeply, the road veering right again and staying on the ridge-line. And as the road cut into the right-hand corner, the land on the left fell away abruptly to give a panoramic view for seeming miles beyond. Still all forest, but at a lower level with similar greens and darker greens and still darker shades further away. Ridges and valleys were untold in number and one could easily get lost if not careful.

Paul and Kalvin stopped at the look-out place and kept an eye on the dogs. Even Tahi now was alert and Bud too had gone away ahead with Spot and Blue.

"Grand view eh Kal."

"Sure is. I could look all day from – where's Blue and them other dogs gone?"

Paul swung back right and peered along the road. Indeed Blue and Spot and Bud were nowhere to be seen, and Tahi was running "harrum-scarrum" to where they had been moments before. Immediately they hurried yonder, and Paul called seconds later, "Come and have a look at this mate."

Kalvin turned back to stare at the ground where Paul was pointing.

"That's fresh-as Paul! Be over 150 too, don't you reckon?"

"At a guess. Sure is a big one and not too old, as you say."

"May as well wait right here I 'spose. Not much point haring off anywhere else, and we're high enough here." Kalvin sat down on the clay bank next to the boar-print they had been looking at, and Paul plumped himself down on a huge wild paspalum plant and looked somewhat like a chook on a nest – very comfortable, with bits of straw and grass poking out all around.

An hour ticked by with no more heard of the dogs except that Bud arrived about a half-hour after he went. He continually looked over his shoulder as he came, and getting to Paul and Kalvin, entirely ignored Mo and Storm and kept on staring into the big bush from where he had come. He was definitely on the alert and must have picked up the scent that the others were working on, but somewhere under the trees had missed the trail. Overshot the turning no doubt in his excitement and couldn't decipher where the pig and the other dogs had gone.

"We'd better head somewhere Paul. I reckon they must have one some place. Look at Buddy, he knows something's up."

"What say I wait up here Kal? You head off where you reckon and yell out if you need me, I may still hear something from up on that knob." Paul pointed ahead a short distance to where a high knoll, covered in short scrub would afford an excellent lookout-cum-listening post.

"Okay, I'm gone. See you back here on the road if nothing transpires." Kalvin disappeared into the shadows of the bush pretty well half-way to the knoll and on the left. Which meant he, Storm and Buddy immediately began a rigorous descent through supplejack and a lot of rimu and taraire trees, rocks and fallen debris making for hard going. It seemed easier for a little while to drop down into the gully more and follow a small trickle of water. There was less supplejack to contend with here and it was pleasantly cool in the damp shade where tiny ferns creviced themselves in chinks of the banks where rock had split, allowing a tenacious hold by their tiny roots.

He hurried on past, getting lower with every stride until well down, a good half-hour from Paul he heard distantly the sounds he had been listening for. Somewhere out to his left there came noises alien to the bush, intruding on his mind vaguely as sounds "not right", and he hurriedly pulled up to listen more acutely. Though he couldn't place them exactly, he knew his dogs were confronting a savage wild pig for the distant barking was ferocious, high pitched and continuous. No small pig would elicit such savagery, ferocity and determination. The prolonged commotion faded minutely as the wind puffed more vigorously every few seconds; and returned to tug inexorably at his mind as he hesitated a few moments, trying to pinpoint direction and distance.

Buddy and Storm had heard too and were gone, so Kalvin simply climbed out of the gully and headed where they had. Up on the ridge a short while later the sounds were more distinct and certain and he upped the tempo as he felt more sure of where to go. Still there was considerable ground to cover and he tore at the impeding shrubbery with a will. Minutes passed and each time he stopped the sounds were louder, urging him on. And not far off now, just over a small ridge he heard a dog shriek, setting off alarm bells in his brain, and he ran again.

In a small hollow as he came stumbling, almost tuckered out, was a sight at once thrilling and filled with dread. Blood-covered ferns and bushes, and a very big pig still quite agile even though held by four determined dogs, and another lying inert at the edge of a huge trampled area. Was it dead?

The boar glared at him as he approached and lunged again when he tried to get close. The din was continual and clamorous, barking from Buddy and deep growling noises from the holders couldn't drown out the snorting and blowing of the black boar. He could see Blue was in a bad way, unmoving, covered in red. So too was Spot, even though he was still hanging onto an ear. Tahi was holding on the side of the jowl, just behind the tusk that had more than likely dealt to Blue. With Spot on the opposite ear and even Mo on his backside it was probably just as well the fresher dogs arrived when they did and took some of the heat off Spot.

Storm arrived the next instant and began to bail as well, darting in where he could to have a nip, and out again to rejoin Bud. Kalvin at last got hold of the boar's back leg and was able to thrust his knife where it did most damage and the enemy quickly became the ex-enemy as he shuddered and knelt slowly on the ground. With no more threat emanating from him as he lay, now pulled onto his side by the still hyped-up dogs, Kalvin wasted no time in inspecting his blue fighter. What a vast relief it was to find him still alive, able even to stagger to his feet and wobble about. Cuts and pokes were everywhere, still oozing blood and Kalvin promptly lay him down again and put his "Swanni" over him to keep him warm and immobile.

Spot staggered over as well and the two of them lay quite thankfully beside the boss and began the long process of getting their wind back, calming down and licking their wounds where they could.

Kalvin hated to think what would have happened had Buddy not alerted them enough to split up, and for him to come down where he had. Even though the tusks were not very big they were sharp as daggers and lethal, as could be easily seen. Tahi had two small rips on one shoulder, nothing to worry about and the others had got off "scot-free". Mo, Buddy and Storm all had blood on them too, though it was not their own, and for this Kalvin was thankful.

Still with his hand on Blue, Kalvin became aware of a voice calling out and yelled uphill for Paul to home in on. Within two minutes his mate turned up and whistled when he saw the 128lb boar and the damage he had done. Pleased he was too at the showing Mo had made and patted his big orange-coloured dog.

"You'll make it yet young fella, good boy! How bad is Blue Kalvin? Spot not too good either. What are the others like?"

"I think they'll all make it. Blue's OK. But ripped to smithereens as well, but nothing real deep thank God. Can you gut the thing for us Paul? I'll try and carry Blue some of the way before I spell you with the pig. Even if it's only a little way. I know your knee won't allow you to do much, but we'll see how we go."

"You know, it's lucky I'm even here," Paul reckoned. "Just once I heard something back behind me and down this way, but I knew it was bailing. Then the wind moved and I never heard anything else. I just decided I'd come down so far and listen again. Course, from half-way down I heard it all, I was pretty well directly above and when you answered me I was pleased I'd come."

Paul got Kalvin's camera and took a photo or seven, one good one of Buddy and Storm as it turned out, and then turned his attention to the two wounded dogs. Fortunately he could pull some penicillin out of his back-pack and gave Blue and Spot a shot each before beginning the long laborious business of gutting the boar and doing the carry part.

Kalvin eventually let Blue down and hefted the pig when Paul's knee told him it was time to have a blow. They stayed on the ridge all the way and broke out onto the road mid-afternoon with an hour and a half at least to the van.

Blue was limping a fair way behind but thankfully had stopped bleeding, and between him and the men Spot hobbled to keep up, still all covered in red but seeming to be okay.

After several rest stops along the way the van hove into view. It was

The enemy quickly became the ex-enemy.

the best, loveliest, most gorgeous van they had ever seen – it represented the end of the long, hard, slow haul – and food and drink while sitting down.

They had to lift Blue into the interior, Spot was able to step up himself as was Tahi, and the three others made it too though not any more full of zest. Kalvin and Paul managed to pull themselves aboard as well, the latter favouring his knee quite noticeably now. He with his limp, and Kalvin with the pig had been pretty evenly matched and only too happy to drive north again thinking of hot chocolate and date scones at Somers' house.

Kalvin hadn't remembered to take the rip collars out of Brett's vehicle this morning and wasn't too keen on hearing his dad's voice after telling him the two best dogs were towelled-up. However, Dad had other things on his mind, he had been in Kaikohe courthouse as a witness or some-such and the case had only been called as Kalvin rang.

"Just give them some more penicillin if Paul's got any left and keep an eye on them. The vet will be closed when you get home. But don't hesitate to get him out of bed if you think they mightn't make it. And take the rip collars next time!"

Kalvin contented himself with a rather meek "Yep, yep, okay." and rang off.

"I think he'll be okay Kal. He seems quite happy lying there on that old carpet. His eyes are bright too. And a big feed of milk and dog-roll will do wonders too I reckon." Paul was genuinely solicitous of Blue's and Spot's welfare and even rang the next day to see how they were.

"Yeah, I took them to the vet early-like just as they opened. They reckoned you did a proper job cleaning them up with that warm salt-water. A real proper job they said – very well done. Just lukewarm was ideal – too hot would probably have led to more bleeding again. You should be a vet yourself mate they said, what with your penicillin and washing out those cuts and rips."

Paul felt pretty pleased himself with praise like that. The dogs felt pretty pleased too, only about eighty stitches between them. Being ripped to smithereens wasn't so bad after all, what with warm milk, plenty of meat and a real fuss being made off them. The only one not too pleased was Kalvin. One good boarnotwithstanding, there was still that vet bill to pay for!

"Way To Go"

The Thursday before Valentine's Day 2002 saw Sam Harris and I on the road to Lake Taupo. This was a previously organised outing to suss out our friend Kieth Hufton's property near the lake. Lucky beggar had gone and bought a 200 acre property down there, a one-time farm, or part of (I've forgotten now) and he let on to Sam that he had seen bare patches of dirt pretty-well at his front door. This front door was on his new "hunting lodge" he'd had built, well off the beaten-track and looking real impressive in "Total Span" design and green "Color-Steel" cladding. With concrete floor and gas cooker, camp beds etc. it was ideal, lonesome, quiet and reeking of hunting atmosphere. There was game of any sort to be taken with rifle, camera or dogs just beyond the ti-tree fringe. And those bare patches of dirt were very revealing. Kieth of "VENISON PORK" fame in the book "*BY TOOTH AND TUSK*" was fairly adept at deciding how these bare patches of dirt came into being. They weren't made by UFOs or aliens, nor by goats with their horns, not even by cows with their hooves, or rabbits either. Something had been out and about for quite some time, and at leisure had dug away or pushed aside the grass for some strange purpose. Yes, he knew all right and he made a telephone call to Sam. Sam had recently pruned Kieth's pines on another property he had at Wairoa and they yarned fairly regularly at the time over "long-distance".

The upshot of all this was Sam and I, "long-distance" notwithstanding, were motoring south in Sam's Hilux with dogs in the box and intending to stay at Kieth and Sheree's place on the North Shore that night.

Next day we were off again, pointing in the direction of Lake Taupo, me and Sam still in the Hilux, and Kieth and son Richard in his late model Jeep. Somehow we got separated from them not long out of Auckland and hummed along at a modest speed talking and conjuring up in our minds what size of hog was likely to have been market-gardening at Kieth's new place.

"Isn't that Porirua Forest country? There's pigs there aplenty so I've heard," I asked Sam. He was driving and glancing more at the hills than the road and came back with –

"You mean Pureora Forest?"

"Yeah, that's what I said."

"No you didn't you stupid galah. You said Porirua."

"What's the difference?"

Porirua's where the mental asylum is or was. You need to be there. Pureora's where the wild pigs are. That's where I'm going, so make up your mind."

"Whatever. Hey, pull up at this dairy. I wanna-nice-cream."

"Your shout," he said as he pulled hurriedly over.

We were somewhere between Cambridge and Putaruru, a small place called Tuakau, Tirau, Titirau or some such. I'd be wrong again whichever I guessed I guess, so just hopped out and ran inside.

We got on the way again a few minutes later licking rum and raisin, and goody-goody gum-drops cones and came not long after to a slightly larger place.

"You bring a morepork with you Reg?" Sam asked nonchalantly.

I looked askance at him (had he completely lost his mind?) Morepork, whatever on earth for?"

"When you go through here you're supposed to drop one off somewhere."

"Wha---at?"

"You DO know ruru means morepork in Maori don't you?"

"Yeah, so?"

"This place is Put- a- ruru. It doesn't say where to put it – I just suppose the post office would do. You sure you didn't bring one?"

I couldn't believe it! Him with all his supposed knowledge about Porirua forests and Tukakaus. He must really think I'm stupid.

"Pu-TA-ruru, you knumbskull. The emphasis is on the TA. You and your blithering morepork. There won't be much of that if you're as hopeless in the bush as you are at place-names."

He smiled (such innocence was hard to believe in a face as ugly as his).

I smiled (mine was superior, as was fitting) and we both lapsed into silence. We'd exhausted ourselves of repartee for a few minutes and simply enjoyed looking into the cool depths of the pine forest as we sped along. There was a lot of that confounded blackberry to be seen and I was keeping my fingers crossed that we wouldn't see too much at destination's end.

For miles then not much was said. And then there was Tokoroa, Dick Lagas' town. This local hunter and I had gone walkabout with his dogs some years ago up a side road and into a forest of blackberry, with the odd pine tree sprouting here and there. It really encouraged me to stay up my end of the country! Blackberry – ugh! But we turned abruptly right somewhere and were on the road to Whakamaru and Taupo's Western Bays. And Waihaha country.

Kieth had told us, "When you come to a good sized river named the "Waihaha", you'll only have a little way to go. About eight and a half kilometres past that there's a yellow gate on the left with a broken top rail. Another two kilometres along you'll see a high hill with bush on top; you can't miss it. Go past about five clicks till you come to Mititau, then turn right onto Briscoe Road and go --."

I couldn't follow Kieth's instructions and was hoping Sam knew where it was. And just as we could see the lake for the first time this idiot in a grey/green Jeep hurtled past giving us the fingers.

No, no! Sorry! It was Richard telling us to follow them. They had just caught up and thankfully were able to guide us to the right place. Man! Were we pleased to see them. I shut the gate and we puttered up a long track to find Kieth and Richard smiling a welcome and stretching, their arms and legs waving about.

"Welcome to Hufton's Safari Park," Kieth said expansively. "Stow your gears in the lodge and tie your curs anywhere you can."

Man! This has to be it! A long shallow valley was spread out before us, but with steep sides all covered in manuka and broom. Some gorse showed itself too and what looked like larger towai trees clung where rocky faces protruded at intervals along the right side. Out there somewhere was the Puri – something forest, crawling with pigs and deer and possums and escaped convicts. A dangerous place for sure but we were keenly anticipating tomorrow's wandering about in that large unexplored (by us) tract of land.

For today, late as it was, we were content to let Kieth and Richard set up camp, while Sam and I went looking for somewhere to tie the dogs up. A good place seemed to be the far end of the valley (nearer the bush as it happened), so we just sort of found ourselves down that way. Sam's Prince and my Rebel instantly showed a marked interest in getting out of sight and we followed hastily, finding ourselves climbing steeply up the right side of the valley. Joe and Jess, my other three as well, also did a marked imitation of pig scouts and we were smiling, sure in the knowledge of the proximity of swine.

It was latish already, the sun well down below the escarpment and Sam suggested we call the dogs in, in case they went "bush" and we not see them again. Thus doing, it wasn't long before they were all back and we headed across to the eastern side which was covered in manuka and second growth bush but had long swathes of grass separating the various patches of scrub. We hoped we'd find something to chase to make the evening interesting (anything found here would have to cross the valley of clear grass) but it wasn't to be, and after another half hour we were back above the lodge. After a steep drop down to the grass we selected spots to tie the seven dogs up and went inside for tea and to discuss tomorrow's safari.

One of the highlights of the trip was certainly Kieth's cooking, and we were fed like kings, yarned till late and finally went to sleep.

Up while it was still pretty dark, I peered outside where heavy fog had descended and everything was drenched in dew. There was no wind and in the darkness everything was as still as the tomb. Nothing moved, nothing murmured, "nothing mate." I had spoken quietly to Sam lest I wake Richard and Kieth. They were in the other room but were stirring a few minutes later and breakfast was on the go soon after that.

It wasn't lingered over though. Hot spaghetti, toast, tea and coffee, cereal and milk had us raring to go in no time. I seem to remember Kieth putting some goodies in a rucksack for lunch way out in Puriri forest somewhere. Come to think of it I don't recall seeing any puriri trees at all – must have the name wrong again.

And right on daybreak we got away. The untied dogs, up until now lying quietly and warm in their nests, became very busy claiming territory, and having to reclaim it again. They all seemed to decide on "that" bush to mark, and "that" tall clump of grass was an obvious choice too, and each dog reckoned it was his. All six dogs were determined to out-pee their peers and the way they went about it you'd swear they had been drinking all night. We hoped any good boar we got onto would have a full bladder too and by the time the dogs had sorted themselves out we were 100 metres up the valley, travelling quick to keep warm.

"What say we check the end of the valley first eh Reg?" Kieth told of seeing a lot of fresh rooting there a fortnight ago and reckoned it was worth checking out.

"Sure thing Boss, you probably know best where to go so we'll just follow you." I dropped my voice and said in an aside to Richard, "That way we can blame him for taking us the wrong way if we don't find a pig eh."

He just grinned as we kept on walking. He and I were supposed to stick together today, leaving his dad and Sam in the other team. Kieth's old Labrador, name of Sam too, was along for the jaunt so we each had four dogs in our team. Sam (the dog) was more astute at finding deer than pigs but hopefully he'd get excited by the bail-up and at least lend a hand with the confrontation by barking and yapping (that's a very definitely necessary part of it all).

The heavy dew would be still on the grass even at ten o'clock. This despite the sun coming up unhindered and unfettered by any clouds at all. Overhead the sky was purplish-blue right now and would only become like that of eggshells later in the day. All around dewdrops glistened, tiny prisms reflecting the sunbeams and turning them every colour of the spectrum. They caught the eye from near and far, sparkling and intense for just that split second and wonderful to see.

What wasn't quite so wonderful was the suspicion of wetness in my socks. I tried to walk last of all, stepping in the footmarks of Kieth, Sam or Richard – anyone who had knocked the dew off the long grass where I was intending to walk. These days I hunted almost exclusively in rugby boots – as a concession to getting long in the tooth. It seems I spend a progressively greater amount of time hanging onto tree-trunks, rocks, vines, whatever, to help me stay on my feet. And the added sure-footedness and lightness sure pay dividends at the end of the day. The downside is getting wet feet at the start of the day when there's dew around. But I'm tough – sometimes!

I was last in line still. Sam and Kieth had got to the far end and were turning back hard right and climbing a little to follow the boundary fence. Richard was a fair way ahead of me too and I cut across the angle to catch up. But of course the others hadn't been that-a-way and by the time I had rejoined the group my feet were wet, wet, wet! All that long grass to push through!

"Joe's gone Reg," Sam whispered as I came up. "Must be a scent around eh. Look at Rebel – and Prince."

Both the dogs referred to had hopped through the fence and disappeared into gorse and broom and fern as he spoke. Maybe something was afoot. With the sun at our backs now, we were on top of a ridge, one that had been bulldozed years ago to accommodate the good eight wire fence that now stood between us and pig habitat. It ran back towards the main highway, passing the lodge half way, though one couldn't see it now, buried underneath the fog lying in the valley.

Up where we were was brilliantly sunny and we could see a long way westwards, out towards pasture in the far right-hand distance, and below us, still shrouded in mist was the river. We could hear the rapids when the breeze dropped a little, and see taller trees on a ridge leading down to the water. But what dominated the vision was the far-flung immensity of the Pari – Piro – Piriroa forest. I was that busy feasting my eyes on the miles of solid green that I wasn't really paying attention to the job at hand.

Just then Richard gasped, a few metres in front of me, and was pointing ahead. "Pigs, Reg, look!"

I looked all right, and saw the last of three whitish suckers duck back into the cover nextdoor.

I seem to remember Sam and Kieth also having seen them and we all surmised there would be a sow not far off. Not wanting to nab her I quickly called Shiney, Tahi and Bud and set off lickety-split for the next rise, careful to make sure the three dogs came too.

We, (Richard and I) stood there quite a while, having to move back a way to "eyeball" the other two, as they had moved in the opposite direction. Nothing happened for what seemed ages – I guess we were all over anxious on behalf of that sow and her young family. That we had moved away was no guarantee she would not be found; and so the time seemed to drag by.

I think Prince came back to the fence and retreated down-slope to where Kieth and his Boss-man were, leaving Joe and Rebel still away. They came too within another quarter-hour and we all heaved a sigh of relief. It didn't last long though. Joe followed Prince back towards Sam and Kieth, Rebel trotted up and along, following where Richard and I had gone, and came to us having missed or ignored the scent of the suckers. But no sooner had he arrived than he leapt clear over the fence, his hackles right up and charged off downhill with all three kennel-mates flat out in his wake. And within fifteen seconds began a ferocious bail only fifty metres away. A snort came too, a yelp, and they were gone.

Richard and I were over that fence too in double-quick time and negotiating as best we could the awful gorse infested terrain where the boar had been found. No sow snorted like that, or was likely to have caused that dog to yelp, besides, we could smell boar now.

The odd bark came from well below us and eventually settled way down towards the river, seemingly in a dirty gut with steep sides. In our haste to get there we found ourselves blocked by a vertical rock face which apparently stretched right and left a good distance. What to do? Richard was right behind me and there was no sign of Sam or Kieth yet. It was up to us two to do the back-up thing for Rebel and co. And as we listened, wringing our hands above the bluff, they sailed on in and a real punch-up began. We could hear all sorts of horrendous noises coming from down in that there fern and gorse and I almost threw myself over the edge. Then I saw it. A slight fissure in the rock wall, one any sane person wouldn't have looked at twice, but we weren't in a position to be contemplating it's feasibility or considering our sanity. I just went over the rim, slithered and slid about ten metres, slowed only somewhat by fleeting hand-holds of fern and tiny shrubs and landed at the bottom in a cloud of dust and debris. I looked up anxiously to where Richard should have been, only to be smacked on the shoulder as he landed (good word) slightly askew behind me. No pleasantries were exchanged, just a look of disbelief and relief between us and we were at the greenery again.

We could even hear mud being splashed around now, only fifty more metres to go – but all alongside a veritable bog. With no chance of edging sideways along the margin, we took to the muddy morass ourselves and floundered around the last corner covered in mud, prickles, pieces of fern and dust and feeling elated at what we saw. Yet exhausted with our run at the same time.

The rivals, locked fast together, were all in the miry water now. The big black boar was far from giving in and lay about as best he could with Shiney and Rebel attached to his ears and the other two harassing him interminably where they could. He stomped about and made the water fly, everything being saturated within five metres, and fern and twigs were crushed down and scattered all over the surface of the creek. It wasn't flowing as far as we could see; a stagnant seep-hole more like, and about a metre deep.

Sam's dogs arrived about then and sailed straight in. Poor old "Boris" was tiring, as indeed we all were, and I looked for an opportunity to get in behind him, up to my knees in muddy water, and end it all. I wasn't too keen on letting the old pig suffer unnecessarily and certainly aren't too impressed by the idea of prolonging the agony just to get

Kieth opens the pig's mouth.

action photos or videos either. If the dogs are bailing, well and good, but where they (and particularly lots of "they") are munching on the thing, or ripping it to bits it's only humane and timely to put the pig down in the quickest possible time. I was utterly disgusted to see one video a while ago where umpteen dogs were besetting an eighty-ninety pound sow, literally mauling it to death, while the hunter leapt around yahooing and sooling the dogs on. This went on for miles too long, the poor pig ripped to bits and dying in absolute agony. Such videos do no good for our sport and ought to be boycotted or banned. I would never buy one – I felt sick all day after and almost sold my dogs. The maker of the video, quite possibly a decent chap in himself, may just never (yet ought now to) have thought over much of the pain such an animal would have endured. I must confess that I once did something slightly similar. In the days when I ran holding dogs I caught a large sow a long way away, and by the time I got there she was almost unable to stand up. In my enthusiasm, (yet unthinking ignorance and stupidity) for letting the thing go, I took the dogs off and got out of it as fast as I could go. On thinking back now I have that same horror. Better by far to have put the sow out of her misery than to have left her to die horribly anyway. I wish now that I had! Hopefully we can all learn!

So I did the proper thing and put him down. Richard's first experience of pig hunting was a boomer. He handled it with aplomb too, sticking with me like he did. And here we had a 130lber to pack out. Kieth and

140

Sam arrived only seconds after the pig had died, before we had time to gut it, and Kieth jumped into the swamp straight off to see what sort of tusks the thing had. Average sized hooks as they were, they nevertheless had inflicted some superficial damage to Rebel and Tahi, but nothing severe.

My footy boots were properly wet now, but worth their weight in gold when it came my turn eventually to have a carry. We had gone straight up the steep incline behind Kieth as seen in the photo where he opens the pig's mouth; Sam having first carry. It was tough going but with Richard and I breaking trail for him it alleviated somewhat the strenuousness of the climb. Kieth next, then Richard and finally myself all carried it at some stage. The good thing about that climb out was that we found an easy grade, once on top, that would lead us next day to the river and became our regular route for the three days we were there – but that's another story.

Coming to the fence at last Kieth shucked his burden, and in the mid-afternoon sun we had a blow, sitting on the grass. It was good to clobber a good boar straight off and we were pretty stoked.

"I'm going to sleep well tonight Dad," said Richy. "Man, that was a lot of fun."

"Me too son, me too. Way to go eh! Way to go!"

I appealed to Sam, "What do you reckon Sam, 130lbs?"

He didn't reply straight away but began nodding his head. And then he tried to sing. (Now, if you've never heard Sam trying to sing, believe me, you don't want to. It's pathetic, truly pathetic!) But this is what he tried to warble his way through (course he was pretty worked up and excited) –

"We are the hunters from way up north,

We really know our pigs –"

Richard and Kieth were rolling around with fingers in their ears and tears streaming down their faces as they stammered "Shut up man. Shut up! Shut up!"

He spluttered a few more words and lapsed into a hurt silence, a look of bewilderment on his face as he glared my way. I was hard pushed to keep a straight face, even for a few seconds so burst out laughing "Ha ha, ha ha ha."

"Wai---ha---ha?" (he ought to have known better).

"Cause you can't sing, and we caught it of course."

A Boar Too Far

Kerry Barfoot of Pouto knew of a place he and I could go hunting on sometime he reckoned. And it was time we went walkabout. I was staying with him while I drove the D7 in the forest and had got talking to the forest manager after having seen the marks of a good boar one day at the side of the road. Wayne Graham knew there were pigs there of course, but not being an avid hunter himself didn't usually pay them much heed.

"They're not usually up this far actually Reg. Could be a loner on the move. Maybe chased from down the peninsula further."

"What about where I'm working at the moment? Seems to be plenty of good cover to hide in?"

"Yeah! There's been the odd one caught out there. But not in that compartment generally speaking. Most of the hunters seem to have more luck where you were last week. Might be worth a look after work if you want to."

But I generally drove the 'dozer til dark, and started next morning before the sparrows were up. Didn't give me much time to be gallivanting about looking for pigs to chase and catch.

And while Wayne didn't have a great deal to give me in the way of up-to-date information on pig whereabouts, he did have something I really did want – but would never get. He was a very keen duck and pheasant shooter and had a lovely black and white male dog which usually accompanied him as he drove through the forest doing what forest managers do. He would come out to inspect my work or tell me where I was to go next and yarn for a little while. This dog would be off the truck and running at full gallop the whole time – you'd have to see it to believe it. He did tell me it's pedigree too once but I have forgotten it now. Though my guess would be a cross between British pointer and some other hound type dog, maybe black Labrador.

I reckoned I could have made an ideal pig dog out of him and offered to give him a kind home if ever Wayne got sick of him. The chances of that though were about zilch. The idea of Wayne going without his dog was about as likely as Wayne going without breakfast. But hang on – Wayne's a big fella (his nick-name is "alligator man") and it is just vaguely possible he may – just may, decide one bright morning to forgo his intake of early morning calories. So you never know. I've got this spare dog-cage ready – may just get a phone call one day.

On lamenting to Kerry over tea that night, he said "Leave it with me a coupla days Reg. I've got to take the digger to so-and-so's place on Thursday and I've got an idea they have pig problems from time to time. I'll ask them and see what transpires."

The upshot of his inquiries was this place referred to earlier.

"I don't know definitely about pig numbers Reg, there's some of course – from time to time. But leave it with me a coupla days. I've got to do some drains out the back next week so I'll scout around and have a look-see for sign."

True to his word, the following week brought good news and bad news.

"Had a look around on Wednesday afternoon, just on knock off. There's sure heaps of rooting and some big rooting too in places. Specially in one paddock next to the pines. But it's a netting boundary fence and I didn't have time to walk in and find his pop-hole."

"That's a shame," I said. "It would be good if we knew where he came and went. It's full moon on Saturday and I'd love to have a go at him by the moon if only we knew where he'd run we'd be able to work the wind good-oh all the better eh."

"Leave it with me a coupla days Reg. I'll check for you on my last day and let you know."

This idea of leaving it with him for a coupla days was growing on me to be honest. The coupla days seemed to have a habit of coming up trumps and so I waited.

I went home up north for the weekend, made sure Olive was behaving herself, not spending too much money and keeping the lawn short and just managed time for a quick walk with the dogs. A medium sized pregnant sow fell to Shiney in the back of Kaeo and I arrived before Tahi and Rebel and co. got on the scene. Shiney has always been under good command and after a couple of "let go" Shiney gave the lucky pig her freedom again and she scampered away. I worried though in that she disappeared in the direction from which Shiney's pack mates were likely to return. It really was her lucky day after all and she lived to have her litter at some time later. More pigs for next year.

Back to Dargaville on Monday morning to drive the bulldozer again. The weather held fine if cold and I got home to Kerry's a mite earlier than him so set about cooking tea. He arrived about 10 seconds after I had finished preparing the meal but he isn't like that. I could hear his voice even before he was out of his Hilux.

"Found his pop-hole Reg. Right on top of the ridge it was. The bad news is he hasn't been back." And as he came in the door he added: "Been some others out further over the hill though. Not quite as big but not too bad either."

"Sounds good mate." I enthused. "Reckon Saturday would be too late?"

"Nah! Should be okay. They said no-one's been chasing them lately. I'm pretty flat-out this week anyway and probably can't get away earlier even if you can."

I had a faraway look in my eye as I answered him: "Yeah, I guess Saturday will do."

The dogs were tied up at Kerry's place during the day and were let off their chains each evening after work. A change of scenery for them seemed to have them all fired up and keen on something. Was it intuition – or what? A new place, a new hunting mate for the boss – a new boar to harass?

We stayed up late-ish on the Friday night discussing strategy. But there's really no such thing. It's just walk behind the dogs and keep your fingers crossed. So we really simply discussed IT. Kidding each other along and ribbing one another on supposed on suspected weaknesses. Kerry reckoned being old (Hey! More mature, mate!) had got to be a real handicap – and he'd wait for me at the top of each hill.

"Cut it out young fella! Us seasoned and hardened stalwarts are all the benchmark you younger jokers have to measure yourselves by. We'll see who waits for who on the tops of the hills."

"Yeah – yeah, we'll see."

"While you've been sitting on your bum all summer, I've been exercising the dogs most weekends. Not hunting I know, but it keeps a bloke reasonably fit. Look at your paunch." He hurriedly pulled his gut in and scowled. "What paunch? Look at yours and all that flab!"

144

Actually neither of us had one – we were just psyching each other out – hopefully. Trying to get or establish a mental edge. But I needn't worry eh? Mental? He couldn't have an edge there could he? I mean to say, just look at that vacant dial of his!

By 11pm we'd exhausted ourselves trying to outdo each other that-a-way and hit the sack. Morning wasn't far away.

It came all too quickly it seemed. Kerry was up and had the kettle on and I looked outside to find a cool cloudless morning on the way. Away to the east the sky way lightening gradually and Kerry's "killers" were already on the move and grazing on a small hillock up near the yards.

"You awake Rebel?" I called.

"Woof, woof." Tahi responded.

"Woof," Rebel added (he didn't talk much – liked to reckon he was all action).

The other two too were certainly awake and pulling at their chains in eagerness to be off.

A slice of bread and jam (two, more like) and a hot cup of Dilmah tea was good enough and we were ready to go.

It was a good threequarters of an hour travelling we did on the way and strangely all was quiet. We didn't talk much and I guessed he was saving his breath for when he had to keep up. Perhaps I'd better not talk either, you never know.

The farmers were up and about when we got there and were happy to engage in conversation a half hour so we didn't get a really early start as we might have. Still, PR is important and so we were happy to listen and talk ourselves when opportunity presented.

But we did get away after a while and set our faces towards the hill. There was a lot of rock around and the track wound in and out and up and over and finally cut through a good sized patch of scrub. Not yet on top though, we weren't looking for sign so were pleasantly surprised to see boar marks heading up the track and disappearing over the side. They weren't too old either maybe sometime in the darkness just past. It could even have been the fellow whose sign Kerry had seen a week ago and we started scanning the forest edge to our right in the forlorn hope of seeing him wandering untroubled back to the bush for the day. But of course he was well gone – we still looked though.

Where would he bed down? Not knowing the area had us at a disadvantage in so far as that we hadn't a clue where the fern patches were, where to look for the nikau groves or where the ridges ran to provide sunny faces. Or the favoured places of the sows, indeed, even which way the forest roads ran – if there were any this way!

The forest edge was scrutinised fairly thoroughly before we headed off under the pines, and along the topmost ridge, going north. Here the grass still grew, how-be-it intermingled copiously with all manner of weeds. Thistles and blackberry and ragwort and tutsin were evident all over and fireweed sprouted in between pampas and hukavine everywhere. The trees were about half grown and it was pleasant enough exploring the bush while keeping an ear out for the dogs.

They worked fairly well when we first entered the trees and were forever investigating old and fresher rootings, trotting here and there, and now and again haring off along some perceived trail.

The sun came out as we found a logging road and so we strolled away along this new ridge, happy to let the dogs work at their own pace. Once, I remember, all four scarpered at the same time ahead of us and rounded the bend. Next second they all came scampering back into view, raced right by and disappeared behind us. We looked at each other kinda wild-eyed. And when ten seconds later the whole four went scampering by again heading the other way once more and in a real hurry I jumped up on a large stump alongside, eyebrows right at the top of my head and what little hair I had left, standing on end.

Kerry busted out laughing – what's so funny?

"Didn't you see it?"

"See what?"

"That bloomin' hare. It was gigantic, raced right past ya man, I'm telling ya!"

"Oh!"

He looked up the road. He couldn't see any great big hare lolloping along. But he did see three dogs trotting back. Seemed to be having fun, so they were. Useless pig dogs! Useless rabbit dogs too. I hopped down off my stump sheepishly and marched off ahead keeping in front of Mr. Barfoot a while. He cleverly stayed behind till something or other claimed our attention and the big vicious hare was forgotten.

In time we found there were no pigs within twenty metres either side of the road and we turned back to give the dogs a chance to venture out to 30 metres. Besides, we were walking into the wind now and we felt lucky for some unknown reason.

Shiney and Bud went left at a water reservoir where the hoof-marks of some 60 pounder showed in the mud at the water's edge. It wasn't fresh sign. But with OUR marvellous pig dogs that was nothing. And so it transpired. They appeared at the corner 100 metres ahead of us and immediately turned away and went over the side again and into a plantation of gum trees. Hadn't even noticed them gum trees on the way up (must have been that blasted hare episode on my mind.)

Omigosh! They weren't going to put that thing up again were they? I stopped and looked over my shoulder. The confounded mind-reader was grinning all over his face. Kerry-blasted- Barfoot was nodding his head and holding his hands out a metre and a half apart. And when he hopped up on the same fandangled tree stump it was just too much. I gave him a salute (not with my hand to my forehead though) and turned away so as he wouldn't see me grin in spite of myself. He soon caught up with me and we glanced sideways at each other – surreptitiously – and started to laugh.

It didn't last long though. The dogs were at work in earnest again. Tahi and Bud leapt up the bank looking very business-like and then Rebel and Shiney did the same and were gone. We kept on at a slow walk up the road listening for the bark. And eventually had to leave the easy walking where it veered sharply right and away from where the hounds had gone.

Rebel appeared first and stayed just a minute before venturing towards that right-branching track we had just left. I watched him as long as I could among the tree trunks but finally lost him in the gloom a hundred metres slightly downhill to the north-west. Kerry was still looking east and listening hard. A rabbit hopped by as we waited. My thoughts went: "A big hare shrunken by fright? – Mind games!"

The open place we were in was the transition between the pine forest and the native bush where the sun shone through and the wind couldn't reach us and we were happy in our waiting.

The trucks on the road way below were a distant sound as were the cattle mooing somewhere downhill a distance. These were just background noises and not paid much heed. Even the tuis calling didn't register over much – we had other things on our minds.

Then a dog barked, and another. Not farm dogs either, even given they were a fair way below.

Kerry looked at me and I nodded. Another flurry of barking had us off into the bush. It was fairly steep here and I was worrying about my ankle as we fought our way downwards. The barking seemed distant now and we stopped to listen again. Yes! They were still on it but moving.

The good old days, Muz, Nick and Jess.

On we went, first one then other in front as we strove to lessen the distance. Big boulders and large rocks among the tree trunks and roots had to be negotiated with care and the lesser light penetrating here wasn't helping a great deal. I was doing a lot of hanging onto branches and smaller tree trunks as opportunity and necessity dictated and getting left behind somewhat. A dog's yelp though spurred me on. In a deepening gut-like depression now we could hear the dogs bailing just around the bend and I paused momentarily. The pig blowing as he charged and the simultaneous crashing and stomping as he was accosted and held were thrilling to hear. Having arrived at that second was rare and wonderful altogether. If he was big and more than a match for the three younger dogs one or more could well have been badly hurt in the ensuing melee and our timely arrival would have been fortuitous. However, Kerry had a hold some fifteen seconds later of a ninety odd pound broken-coloured pig, a boar certainly with half-grown hooks and was grinning again.

I delivered the coup-de-grace in time to avoid any wounds to the hunters and sat down to recover my breath. The shade we were in seemed compounded by the wetness of the place, and I recall water-ferns aplenty and a small mill nearby. All cool and shaded, the area we were in was virgin bush and untrammelled by humankind or stock – until now. And because of where the dogs had run him to ground we surmised the boar had simply been passing through and been apprehended, unluckily for him. Or he may have been asleep in the sunlit glade we waited in and been found that way. Who knows?

I gutted the pig fairly soon and putting it on Kerry's back made off slightly downhill towards the faint noise of traffic on the highway. A deepish side-gully with water in it was traversed almost immediately and then more easy going appeared until we fell out onto another forest road some three or four hundred metres along. Now this is where the story really begins.

A discussion ensued as to which way we ought to turn. Kerry was adamant that we should turn right and head (he said) to a gate which probably wasn't all that far away.

I was aghast! Had he no idea at all? You only had to re-run our route in your mind to see he would be on course for the far end of the forest.

"Oh c'mon Kerry. That'd even be heading away from the traffic you can hear. We've got to go left. You'll see! Trust me."

He looked pretty sceptical and offered some more reasonable argument re going opposite to my way out. But it wasn't vehement, or even as forcefully stated as my reasoning and at last shouldered his burden and began the long tramp out.

We covered about a kilometre in silence, stopping only once when Rebel seemed interested in heading up a ridge on our left. His nose was up, and he was winding just prior to leaping up the bank. Gorse and other low scrub swallowed him up pronto and it wasn't long before the other three headed off too. We waited, regaining our breath somewhat in the interval and still not saying much. We had been climbing gradually, pretty well since we started and this had me perplexed a little. The continual winding in and out of gullies and across ridges really ought to be descending by now. There was undoubtedly a major ridge ahead that we had to cross before dropping to the getaway and we were almost there now.

The appearance of the four pig dogs trotting our way from the front convinced us it was time to push on. Whatever had interested them obviously hadn't been caught up with – maybe down low in the underbrush the scent couldn't penetrate as easily as on the open road and so they had lost it.

Gradually Kerry got to his feet and began again. Another kilometre went by and he looked pretty weary as we changed over. I had noticed his steps going a mite slower the last half kilometre. We were still climbing and I reckoned it was only fair that I have a go at carrying it a while. By the time we had done the third kilometre I was pretty convinced something was not as it should be.

"This idea of yours is just plain dumb Kerry. Any twit can see you should have listened to me in the first place – we've wasted all that time and effort for what? There's no gate for yonks this way I reckon. We'll just have to give in and go back," I didn't look at him as I said this.

He coughed and spluttered – twice, and came up with "Yes, you will have to won't you."

Shaking my head melodramatically, I turned around with the pig still on my back and began the three kilometre downhill stretch. Changing roles gave us each a breather every little while and after a "lifetime" arrived back at the spot of our emergence from the bush. We were pretty tired by now and so very thankful for the almost continual decent.

"The gate is only a half kilometre at the most I reckon Reg. This road will take us around the head of this gully here and then it'll drop a few hundred metres around several corners and we'll be there." Kerry was somewhat recovered now and lifted the boar for one last carry. My knees were a bit wobbly and I felt pretty tuckered-out actually and fell in behind Mr Barfoot. The proximity of the gate (now that I had convinced him of it's proper direction) seemed to give us just a little bit more bounce as we headed down. And even before we got there we could see farmland beyond the tree trunks that were becoming gradually fewer and eventually petered out as we rounded a last right-hand corner to find an open forest gate before us.

We hid the boar in the scrub not far away and putting strings on the dogs, headed south along the tarseal for another kilometre. The yellow Mitsubishi truck was a welcome sight to be sure and even Rebel, Tahi, Shiney and Bud seemed keen to hop up and settle in their box after such a big walk.

Driving back to secure our pig saw us in good spirits once more and the verbal jousting got under way again.

"Lucky one of us had the brains to sort it out eh Reg."

"Don't give me that crap. If I hadn't suggested turning around we'd have been still walking uphill."

"Good try Reg, good try," I wasn't fooling him at all, just saving face a little – maybe.

As we lifted the boar onto the truck some tourists pulled up and Kerry and I posed for photographs headed for Switzerland. Those photos would go a long way eventually and I thought it quite appropriate. Our own photos when developed would remind us too of the time we carried a boar too far.

" I don't know Clive, but these things really give me the creeps! "

First Time Success

During the time I was living at Kerikeri I found it handy to hunt somewhere close, rather than go all the way up to my usual stamping grounds. In a conversation with Sam Harris I mentioned a new place I had found (new for me I mean) and he immediately informed me he had hunted there a couple of times or more with his friends Sam and Leo Kidd already. I thought I was going to let him in on my new secret place and he really burst my bubble with this confession. Still, he had hunted another part of the bush from where I had made a bridgehead and I guessed it wasn't likely we'd get anywhere near his area so it would be new country for him.

It was in fact very hard country for the dogs to pull up a pig in. Here again it was gorse and of course, more gorse. Scattered throughout were patches of native bush, manuka, pine, wild passion-fruit, flax, gums, wild ginger – in fact, you name it, and it was bound to be there someplace. And seeing that I hunt most of the time in the gorse, my dogs were used to it and instantly at home. I'd love to go somewhere where there's a lot more native bush and less gorse, where the cover is a bit less tight for I like to think my dogs would love it and go all right. I reckon I'd love it too.

Anyway, Sam was keen for a run on Saturday morning and agreed to meet me at the junction around 6.30am. I kept a weather eye on the forecast and was a little apprehensive when the man said there was a possibility of heavy rain for the far north. Though it wasn't a probability, the very thought of getting wet was nearly my undoing. I don't remember exactly how many times I've been caught out, sometimes miles from the vehicle and without any sort of a raincoat at all but it's been a few. Nowadays I carry a two dollar poncho or plastic throwaway slicker in my gear, but of course these get ripped pretty easily when in the thick

A large sow turns to thank Des Sands for her freedom.

of it. A butterfly-cape or bushman's cape is ideal. It can be worn all day or even wrapped around one's waist or rolled up in a pikau or backpack. Being open at the front lets you perspire and the air flow better than with a "Swanni" or coat, besides, it's super good when you've got a pig to lug out. It stops you feeling uncomfortable with all that blood on your back or soaking your undies.

It's my usual winter attire and as this was winter, I had it ready in the truck as I loaded the dogs in the dark. Rebel, Tahi, Shiney and Bud were all relatively young and still learning (like me – young and still learning). At least the still learning part is true. Rebel was three and a half and Tahi, the brindle and white Staffi cross was two and a half while Shiney and Bud were only about fifteen months old. Not a super-duper pack by any means even if Rebel in particular was doing okay.

Sam's dogs were much the same age. Joe and Jess were from the same parents as Rebel though a year younger and of the two Joe was shaping really well. He learned a great deal I think from Prince who was a top notch stopping dog with only one vice. He tended, once the pig was stopped, to wreck the thing's nose and consequently Sam wasn't having much success at releasing pigs unless he got there pretty fast.

Well, here we were, having met as arranged and motored on to my entry point. This is kept a secret even yet – for obvious reasons. It saved a lot of travel to the main entrance where there were a lot of signs. Pictures abounded of vehicles, fires, motor-bikes, guns, dogs etc all with a big red stripe through them. I'm not too sure what that red stripe meant, but guessed that seeing Tahi had brindle stripes, that would be near enough and we were "in." But petrol and diesel are expensive, so we saved all that extra travel and hoofed it from my "posi". Only trouble was we had to fight our way through a lot of gorse before we hit any decent sort of going. But there were compensations.

The rain had come to nothing and as we left the vehicles the sun had just shown over the treetops eastward.

"Looks like being a good day after all eh Reg."

"Yeah, does, doesn't it."

"D'you mind waiting a minute? I'll duck back and leave my raincoat at the truck."

"Me too," I reckoned. "I really don't think there'll be any rain so I'm just going to wear my nylon parka." The pockets were good to carry camera and string etc and the whole caboodle was lighter by far at the end of the day than my butterfly cape or Sam's "Swanni".

Within ten minutes we were back at the farm gate and disappearing into the tall trees on a track that led downhill. Cattle had been here recently, and pigs, for we could see the hoofmarks of both. Unfortunately the beef animals had trampled all over the signs made by the bacon animals and we were hard put to it to decipher what hogs had been working the ground here.

Prince and Joe were already gone, out to our left somewhere and we kept an ear and an eye out for the pair of them. But with the wind coming from our right we didn't think it likely they had smelt pigs already, unless it was some lingering odour on the ground.

"Unlikely I reckon, but you never know." Sam voiced my own opinion and I nodded as I watched Tahi. Well, maybe not so unlikely. My number two dog was certainly getting keener by the minute. It only needed Prince's bark to have him off and flying, feet hardly touching the ground as he sailed over fallen trunks and branches, homing in on where Prince and Joe both barked spasmodically. Their pig was moving in a hurry and only their intermittent barking told where the chase was at. Below us in the direction they were headed was a creek, not deep but downhill a good way through fairly open going and as yet we were standing still and listening "like all get-out". Bud had gone with Rebel and only Shiney was absent on the other side of the ridge we were on.

I imagined the pig, desperate to get away, putting distance as best it could between where it had been found and where it was now. Careering upstream, listening even as it ran, for the pursuers on it's trail. Were they closing the gap inexorably, bringing death with them? The hateful hounds would have no mercy should they be successful and he strove even harder, endeavouring to lengthen the lead on that awful black and white dog that had disturbed him from his rest. His alarm was heightened by an ominous panting behind him only a little way. On his trail yet they were, four-footed and imminent. Peril behind, danger coming apace, safety where? If only he could out-last them. On he went filled with horror – yet hope too. Just now the blood – curdling baying behind was further aft it seemed – just a little.

We heard it too, up towards the gum trees yet still in the gully. The boar, undoubtedly a boar, was climbing fast, the barking less frequent, the intervals longer and the chase slowing according to our perception of it. You can't catch them all and a short while later Sam grinned, smiling, yet with chagrin etched there too.

"Looks like he's got away Reg."

"I guess."

One lone bark away high on the skyline was all we heard after that. Down on the last grassy patch near the creek we waited – and waited. Still we waited. With five of our dogs gone it was pointless going further at that stage and as each one turned up the lack of injuries of any sort told of never really having got close.

One light-hearted boar, tired no doubt but singing in his heart his freedom song, trotted on a long way, exhilarated by his escape from jeopardy and despair. Alert nonetheless, for all the bush was fraught with danger when dogs were about, he was now only being cautious. It would be some time yet `ere he retraced his steps, and he was happy to wander wide and far feeling illustrious, for hadn't he vanquished his pursuers. Those dogs doggedly on his trail, doing their best to intercept him had succumbed at last to his superior fitness and his astute use of his terrain. That he had out-climbed them spoke volumes in itself for these weren't your average or run-of-the-mill pig dogs. Either Prince or Joe, veterans of umpteen battles and trails were quite capable of persevering over long distances and of strenuous pursuits to finally nail their adversary. They'd had finally to concede defeat, and returned well on towards midday, tongues lolling and panting, non-stop, apparently pleased to flop down and rest a while.

Joe, standing like the hero he was.

Sam and I stayed put, giving the last dogs (Prince and Joe) a bit more time to recover. Rebel and Tahi had come back a long time previous, never really having caught up with the chase and were well rested, but even so, we reckoned (or hoped) for another extended pursuit culminating next time in victory. Naturally we would rather a shorter run (even better, a catch in a pig's bed) though there's not much excitement there. But peradventure we had another longer chase we'd need those more experienced hounds and their acumen in the pack. (We must have known something). Rebel could easily do it by himself, but no dog is infallible, and where he might miss a turning, Joe or Prince may possibly pick it up and save those precious few seconds. And an extra finder or two wandering about in the scrub, enhanced our chances of a strike. The more dogs one has does not necessarily mean a merrier day and especially not so in a battle where they impede each other in a sudden charge, or get in each others way in the scuffle, even at the bail with other dogs arriving, will sometimes alarm a pig enough to make it break again.

This though, a vast jungle of nearly impenetrable gorse would require every bit of finding expertise we had on hand. A good number of times I've carried on, not waiting for a lesser dog to arrive after a futile chase, knowing it would come eventually anyway, and being still a learner,

A 100 pounder keeping her feet dry at Sam's expense.

probably not contribute to a successful bail by the better ones in the team. This was the reasoning behind our continued lazing in the sun.

Eventually, after the sides of the main dogs had stopped heaving a quarter hour or so we got to our feet and crossed the small stream. I remember deciding to leap across, and fell in, on discovering the far bank was undermined. A wet foot wasn't going to be all that exciting for a while but was endured stoically in the anticipation of the better good! Sam made it ok (darn it all), and we set off up a vague avenue I thought I perceived in the dense cover confronting us. I had gone that way previously, breaking branches and gorse stems but that was some time ago and now I was hard put to it to figure out a way ahead. Leather gloves came into their own here, but even so on a very rare occasion a spike would find a seam where the stitching was maybe a shade open, or loose, and give me a moment of intense feeling. Sam had the enjoyment, I had the pain. But conversely, now and again, I'd hear him yell "ouch!" – and I'd snigger to myself. "That'll teach you to laugh at me when it's my turn." But he's tougher than me (according to Sam Harris – and generally didn't let on. Something I reckoned about less pain indicating less – less – I have heard the saying, somewhere! Once!

Eventually we came out onto a bush track of sorts and turned left towards where the earlier chase had petered out. Now, just after midday the sun was pretty warm and we were wearing our possible-wet-weather-gear tied around our middles. We sauntered on and watched a trio of magpies playing chasey, their black and white plumage flashing alternately in the sunshine as they flew not far overhead. A big circle above the pond on the left had them streaking back towards us, cawing all the while, ducking and diving in an abandon of élan. A bit early I guess for courting, perhaps a threesome of juveniles just enjoying themselves in the heat of the day. They disappeared behind us as we ascended a small hill, fortunately going the same way as the track we were on.

We could see a fair way into the distance now, mostly gorse's brilliant yellow and green, and while this meant there should be a few pigs around, we weren't terribly excited at the prospect of getting among it in a hurry. So we decided to explore further along our track, heading we hoped for some native bush, or more open manuka. The cover however remained gorse, some bigger gums here and there and now a lot of medium-age pines. Judging by the number we could see from the top of a small rise, we were into somebody's pine forest up here and so kept an eye out for someone whose pocket we could pee in if necessary. But no one came.

It was getting on to one o'clock now and we were thinking of stopping again to chew on a muesli bar and have an apple. We had pretty well decided on a patch of long roadside grass just ahead (We were on a dinkum road now) to rest on and hadn't noticed our intrepid four go bush a few yards back. A count of dogs as we lay down alerted us to the disappearance of said hunters and we immediately stood up, suspicious again. Especially when the remaining three decided to head off all together that instant, diving downhill over the edge into a big valley laid out to the west. And sure enough a bark came not long after and we were full of adrenalin again, rest forgotten, apples and muesli hastily stuffed into pockets, already sizing up options. Ahead that broad valley of pines, further over another ridge dark green with the same species and away on our left a skyline ridge with similar vegetation except for a high clay slip facing us as we gazed all around.

The dogs this time were more bunched up, Joe and Prince (hard to tell their voices apart) had found another good one. I heard Rebel too and even Tahi was close enough to sound off. Those four together weren't likely to fail we reckoned and confidently headed uphill at a run.

But after breasting the top of the hill we stopped to find only silence from out yonder. Flabbergasted, we didn't know what to make of it. In the time it had taken us to puff our way to the summit, we supposed they would have pulled their pig.

"I reckon we should go further round Sam. They're probably gone over into the next valley and we can't hear them," I managed the whole sentence in one long rush – and gasped in air once more.

"No, wait a sec! Ah, you're right."

Sam had indeed heard something, and supposing (wrongly) that I had too, was off like a greased rocket (I've never seen, or heard of one, but I reckon it'd be fast – and have difficulty catching Sam at that). I ran too, playing catch-up (and was getting further behind). Until Sam stopped again at another junction, head thrust forward and hand held up to shush my scuffing on the gravel as I came up. A distance of twenty metres separated us and I was only just getting my breath back when he was off again, pounding down that track on the spur heading back north. I followed now like a second rate pig dog. Knowing something was going on but not exactly what, following the leader and hoping like crazy he knew what he was about.

I did actually gain on him on the down-slope and was congratulating myself when he suddenly dived off the track and began to "bush-bash" frantically towards a sound I could now hear vaguely coming from a fairly deep and steep gully down below where no pines grew. Manuka was more noticeable and as we got lower, so was the noise. No bailing but a steady, clamorous and heart-stopping battle was in progress and we still weren't there. An occasional yelp from a dog told of wounds and a mind-numbing shriek seconds later filled us with dread. We knew a boar was doing his darndest not far away, ripping into our dogs apparently quite effectively.

Down we went pushing at the ti-tree, leaping gutters and obstacles, smashing greenery aside and came at last to see what we were there for. Opposite us on a small ledge (for want of a better word, a black boar of around about 110lb was being held by our bailers. Five of them had a smattering of pit-bull in them and in the heat of battle this tended to show itself in the readiness of our dogs to hold where they thought they could.

Tahi, mostly Staffordshire Bull Terrier was in there too and only Prince had no known heavy breed in his heritage. But hang on, he came from Kiwi, who came from Rover, who came from Blue – ah, there it is. She was from an English setter X Bulldog, out of a Boxer-Doberman. Heavy breed enough to ensure his frenzied participation here.

A small creek flowed between us and was crossed not even realising it was there. With my knife out I made a grab for the pig and a minute later it was all over. The water continued to spill and splash down the rock face and gurgle away, and became a boon in the washing of hands, knives etc. The large rock was put to good effect as a place to photograph the 102lb boar. Joe got in on the act too standing there like the hero he was, pretty pleased with himself I'm sure. We were too, with all of them in fact, me with Sam and him with me (I think). There were no serious wounds on any of the dogs after all. Just a few gashes and small rips and pokes here and there. And on such a high note we'll leave the story there. The carry out and the long haul home was really just like any other and we fell asleep at home still smiling.

Second Time Too

We had found out the name of people who had jurisdiction over the forest we were in a couple of weeks ago and I had intended approaching them for a permit, (or permission to enter the place in the pursuit of wild pigs). But being the world's best procrastinator (as regards some things) I hadn't got around to it.

Sam had gone with Des somewhere last Saturday and caught a couple of smaller pigs. One was let go but they had to kill the other and took it home for the larder.

"I'll bet there's another boar or two in that patch of grass Reg and I hunted in a fortnight ago," he told his girlfriend Jodi. "I'll give him a ring later and see how he's placed for tomorrow."

She was going to see her mum and dad at Maungatapere and wouldn't mind at all Sam excercising his dogs further North and a short time later he rang me at the Youth Camp in Cooper's Beach.

"Hey Reg, I'm going to go and catch another big boar in Siberia tomorrow. You able to come too?"

"I think so. I'd better come and keep an eye on you in case you cross the border into Asia and get picked up by the authorities. What time?"

We made arrangements to meet fairly early and then tried hard to get to sleep, knowing it could be a long walk in the morning.

The morrow arrived all too early for the sleeping Reg and not early enough for Reg the hunter. He tumbled out of bed and grabbing a torch went outside in the mothy dark.

Bugs and other flying things of all sorts were about in the pre-dawn darkness – not a good sign. And as a heavy drop of rain smacked me on the shoulder I hurried back inside to ring Sam. Not much point really so put the kettle on, and resigned myself to the distinct possibility of getting wet some time later on. Sam would come anyway and give me cheek about getting old or not being tough enough or some such crap. I'd show him, the young upstart. When I was his age –.

Breakfast this morning was simply four slices of toast and Marmite, a hot cup of Bournvita and a few malt biscuits. I couldn't waste too much time as Sam was nearly always early and I had yet to get everything and everyone aboard and still do three quarters of an hour's drive back to the crossroads.

The cold June day gradually appeared with an east wind bringing in drizzle from towards the lightening sky. And yes, Sam's grey Hilux was waiting for me and I tooted as I drove past, and watched the rear-vision mirror to see him start to follow. His lights came on as he moved off, mine were on "dip", and were needed less and less as we drove the remaining kilometres to our parking area.

The light drizzle falling as we got out had Sam turning up his collar and frowning out to sea.

"I wish the sun would come out. Don't like this miserable stuff". He wasn't happy for some reason — not like his usual cheery self at all. I was going to needle him a little, but decided to keep my mouth shut, murmuring something like "Me either mate, me either."

Dogs were released, rip-collars donned, rifles slung etc and as we headed down the bush track under the canopy of the leaves, it became apparent that the drizzle had given way to a steady rain. Glad I was to have brought my cap and we soon had the parkas of our nylon jackets up over our heads, the peaks of our hats keeping the water out of our eyes. And once out of the cover of the trees the wind hit us too. How it could change so suddenly and in such a short distance was amazing. We were feeling pretty "down in the mouth" and glancing sideways at each other as we walked along, hoping the other would say "Let's chuck it in eh? Let's go and have a hot pie at the dairy."

I didn't and Sam wouldn't, even though he wanted to. He imagined I thought he was tough and daren't let me have any inkling he maybe wasn't quite so. I actually do, and think he's a grand mate, but I was secretly hoping commonsense would prevail and he'd come out with "Reg –."

"Yeah, too right mate, I agree, lets get out of here."

Whereas he was going to say "Reg, where did you get that new knife from?"– maybe – and I would have got sucked in. But he never said it.

We arrived at the bottom flat or grassy paddock bordering a little creek that trickled alongside at low tide.

And suddenly my mate changed, just like the weather, for right in front of us was irrefutable evidence a big pig had been a-grubbing. In an instant he was all animated, darting here and there, on tenterhooks as he watched the dogs seriously at work quartering the ground. Rebel leapt the small watercourse and disappeared poste-haste scrubwards. Prince was next, then Shiney. Where they all crossed over must undoubtedly be where the hog had gone, leaving his scent for them to follow. Tahi, Jess and Bud were only seconds behind too, all critically intent on the trail before them. We in turn, serious and elated all at once, crossed the flat ground and jumped over onto the devil-weed infested far bank and immediately turned left, and seconds later had gone from view. Our track, a bit more open than two weeks ago had numerous pig-runs crossing at intervals and we inspected each one as we crossed. Supremely confident of a chase at any moment, we pushed for the top road. Pig marks of all sizes showed on these crossings and we knew it was only a matter of time before the dogs would open up. Hiding somewhere underneath all that dense cover was our pig just awaiting our finder to winkle him out and start him off.

We burst out onto the road (if it could be called a road) and stood listening expectantly. Ten minutes had gone by since we had changed our disposition back on the flat paddock, since the dogs had changed from lethargic disinterest to galvanised action, since the wet stuff had changed from drizzle to rain. All was changed. And now the weather changed again. The rain was no more and a weak sun was trying to peer out from between the clouds, which were scooting away behind us. All was well in our world, except for the lack of barking.

The sign was so fresh, but with the rain and all, we could have been deceived, possibly the dogs too. But their keenness belied the idea of no scent at all and we were still wondering about it all when most returned. Only Rebel and Joe remained absent and we pushed on towards the main forest road a kilometre ahead. Listening as we went we fully expected the return of the two remaining dogs any moment as Prince and Tahi had already come back and Prince in particular wasn't likely to be quickly thrown off the trail very readily. It was only a matter of time.

It was too, a long time! The wind had dropped even more and the sun shone bravely if not too warmly, as even now more clouds seemed to pile up on the horizon.

Not knowing where Joe and Rebel were, we decided to keep going in the hope Prince and the others put up a pig by themselves. This could bring the other two in from wherever they were, besides, on climbing further we might just hear them yodelling well over the skyline.

While the mood was lighter now there was nevertheless that small niggling worry over our finders being not with us and the small talk reflected this from time to time.

"I wonder where that road goes? Seems to go in the right direction" mused Sam, as he looked at where our road became an intersection. We were well up now, pretty well on top of the main ridge, the exact same spot we had been two Saturdays ago when we were hurriedly deciding where to go to "home in" on the dogs chasing the 102lb boar caught near the small waterfall.

"Probably the main road back towards Leo's area I guess." This from me, as we approached the junction. No dogs were ranging ahead for once and we just ambled slowly uphill.

Quite suddenly all changed again. In a split second it seemed Rebel appeared right where the three roads met. There he was streaking across our bows flat-out. He had come from over the edge of the road, appearing as if by magic and totally ignoring us, strove mightily to close the gap between him and the great broken-coloured boar scarpering just three metres in front of him. Not a sound came except the urgent scattering of gravel as the big hog sprinted for the scrub on the other side. To this day I don't know if any of the "at heel" dogs knew a thing about it. Perhaps they were too low down to see over the rise. But Sam and I both saw and stood transfixed, mouths agape momentarily at the spectacle just witnessed. But they disappeared faster then they had come. A brief five or six second cameo enacted before our eyes, totally unexpected and totally thrilling too. Totally galvanising as well, for next second Sam and I burst into action. Five dogs from behind us, alerted by our body language, rocketed past, hit the junction and turned sharply left in a disorganised jumble of legs and madly sniffing noses. Rapid acceleration was next as they all decided to overhaul Rebel and his boar, and they too disappeared. We ran there too, and saw the marks at a log-landing area where all had dived over the side and into the thick gorse once more, and we were left alone to listen again.

Alone that is except for Rebel. He came to us then, walking slowly and panting as he struggled up. I sat down and hugged him for a few seconds but he wanted to move away and totter around a few metres off, hyperventilating it seemed – panting with tongue lolling all over, and rubbery legs doing their best to keep him upright. It only lasted a half-minute and he flopped in the shade at the edge of the road and remained there as all the other dogs came back one by one. We never

Bud was extremely fast and savage.

heard any more of the broken-coloured one, haven't yet crossed his path again and we were left wondering how far Rebel had chased him. Was he the original pig? Where was Joe? How come the pig had escaped again? Why hadn't the other dogs smelt him coming?

While we were talking and trying to find answers, a brown dog appeared from around the last corner downhill and trotted up.

"Joe! Where have you been old fella? What happened? You tired too? Never mind, next time you'll get him won't you old chap." Sam was making a fuss of his dog, clearly pleased at the outcome, regardless of the "no pig" situation. And that happens periodically doesn't it. It would be folly (not to say down right untruthful) to claim a 100%, even 90% success rate when in the bush and we sat and rehashed the morning's run philosophically. Another time, another pig.

Little did we realise our "another time" was just around the corner, not an hour away.

"Let's head for home eh? The dogs are stuffed, I'm tired and it looks like it might rain again." We'd had a run and I was satisfied – sort of.

We both had had enough really and the thought of hot chocolate and a hot pie rather appealed just then. Those cumulus clouds building out to sea would later in the afternoon bring rain again for sure. Especially if the wind got up, as well it might.

We got to our feet, called the dogs and began the long slow shuffle home. Around a few corners a side-road to the left angled off on a nearly flat gradient and sported a sign declaring this was Fantail Road.

Sam turned left stating a little self-consciously: "May as well have a quick look down here, it can't go very far I would say, you keen?"

"Yep! May as well see where it goes!"

There wasn't much in the way of drying in the air and while we were comfortable as we walked along it wouldn't take much to have us pretty wet. A few minutes rain, even a fifty metre dash through the scrub would suffice. Some moisture must have evaporated I suppose but there was probably enough left to saturate at least the person in front. We thought our hunt was over for the day though and were just exploring. This was the country Rebel must have come through, maybe even Joe too, and probably there were no pigs for miles.

Who barked first I don't know now. We were strolling along one minute and standing stock-still the next as we listened to an almighty shindig erupt down in the valley we had our backs to. Obviously a pig of no uncertain size was angry at being disturbed and was telling the dogs to lay off and stop bellowing in his ear.

"Here we go again cobber, you ready?"

"Wait a sec' Sam, wait till Tahi and Bud get there too." These last two were the only ones we saw after the initial set-to. They shot across our bows at ninety miles an hour – had been in the opposite basin and now mad-keen to join the battle with a daddy-oh pig. They never saw us for all the indication they gave, eyes fixed steadfastly on the wall of scrub in front, back legs reaching way past their snouts in an endeavour to get there even faster. And arrive they did. Joining the other five gave them all "Dutch courage" and they sailed in forthwith. We heard the upshot of all that determination. A scream, a few second's silence, and a pounding of feet/hooves interspersed with a yip and a yap, a "woof" and "wif-wif" told of our boar absconding to greener pasture, or thicker jungle. No more then twenty metres behind us up the track this jet-black pig raced across and hurled himself into where Bud and Tahi had been. The whole seven dogs were right on his hammer and we knew he wouldn't get far.

"Whew! See that? Man! did you see it? Good pig man, and good hooks too I reckon. Come on!" Sam was off like a hairy goat in the wake of the dogs. You could still hear them yakking as the trail led lower and lower towards the gutter. Fainter and fainter it became and then petered out, leaving us in the middle of nowhere, ears straining and hearts pounding. A look of disbelief was definitely justified till we thought of our jaded main dogs and then replaced by one of disappointment. The dogs had been so "on" him he simply couldn't get away could he? Being around 120lb to 130lb he was in his prime, disgustingly fit, furious too and fleet of foot. I personally guessed that if anyone was to pull him up it would have to be Bud or Tahi. For Prince, still in his prime never appeared over-fast to me. He was Sam's dog and I never really knew how fast he was. Shiney was too fat and unfit, Jess was young and inclined to return after a short chase, and Joe and Rebel were already tired after their epic run an hour or more ago. I knew too that Bud was extremely fast and savage when truly riled. The whippet and pit-bull in his makeup showing in these circumstances and so I was still hopeful. Until he returned (he was inclined to be like Jess on occasions and chucked it in too early) I never gave up hope. Tahi was coming into mid-age and was very fast too, probably fitter even than Bud and certainly more experienced. And this was the third time today a boar had teased them. Surely they would stick it out for once and haul in their prey.

"Just keep going Sam. We'll hit the main road if we go straight ahead and climb this ridge."

"Probably right. It's shorter than going back anyway."

We pushed on relentlessly. Not half as wet as we had imagined it to be, the scrub was very matted and thick where we were and we took turns at trail-blazing a good twenty minutes.

A two metre drop onto the gravel road came suddenly and with a sigh of relief I slid down. Not Sam though, he was off and running immediately after jumping past me and haring off down the road. Now I know I'm a little – well – maybe more than a little deaf, but I was darn sure I could hear no barking. Reluctantly I "geared-up" the legs and tried to keep Sam in view but he was perceptibly gaining ground in front of me. Suddenly he stopped, spun around to see if I was coming and waved his arms excitedly, pointing ahead again. Then off he galloped once more and I was just in time to see him slip into the pines growing alongside the left-hand edge of the road. Too far away to yell, I simply ploughed on till at the point he had gone bush and pulled up to listen.

Yep! He had heard it all right. The dogs had their pig a quarter kilometre into the pines, downhill, but in the direction of home. I knew I could afford to slow down a little now. I even stopped a couple of seconds to have a blow. I hope Sam doesn't ever find out – he would be

Sam, taking our 120lb boar the last few yards.

relying on me to back him up if need be. Well, I would – soon.

Halfway there the sounds were unmistakable and thrilling. The tempo was flat-out and furious and by the sounds of it not all the dogs were holding. A terrific ruckus was certainly going on but I heard the change in the clamour as Sam arrived. He had hopped in smartly behind the boar, black as black again, and wrapped the long bristly tail around his hand. They were all in a tight thicket of ferns and devil-weed and moving slowly down-gut. Behind, they had left a broad swathe of flattened undergrowth where the pig had endeavoured to loose the dog's holds with his thrashing around and sudden lunges where he could. Prince was doing wonders on his snout, never letting up a second hampering to some considerable degree the boar's ability to hook Rebel, Tahi and Bud on his ears. The steam rising all around was evidence of the intensity of the battle and antagonists all were giving their utmost to come out on top. Jess, Shiney and Joe all had a mouthful most of the time, under a leg, on the jowls – wherever. He did notice however, that

Sam's wife Jodi, with the beast.

as soon as he arrived Jess was happy to relinquish her claim to being a holder and returned to her bailing duties up alongside Prince. Poor old black and white dog would need earmuffs if this carried on!

Sam began to relax now, Reg would come past any second and stick the thing for him. But no! Reg wasn't coming. Maybe he was still up at the road. He would have to do it all himself – so did. The boar, vanquished for sure, settled slowly, probably not even realising he was dying and rested his chin on his front legs as the "Prince" flopped to rest alongside. The dogs knew the fight had gone out of him in no time at all and were thankful too to be able to stagger around. Wobbling and tottering about, they lurched and reeled around finding someplace they could lie down and pant and shut their eyes. They must have had it maybe twenty minutes and in that time had been fighting non-stop at full strength. No wonder they were exhausted and tuckered out.

Sam realised he was pretty "had it" too and lay back yelling out "Down here Reg," and shut his eyes.

I appeared about a minute afterwards, looking for a scene of battle and found instead seven dogs, a man and huge black pig all asleep in the middle of the jungle. Quick as a flash I thought of gutting the pig, putting it on my back and marching off leaving them all to snooze a while longer. What consternation there would have been on waking.

"The b– pig has 'come to' and shot through while we slept." Such would be the surmise in all their minds. But there wasn't much chance of that. Before I even fully arrived dogs had stirred, opened their eyes and I could see even Sam was smiling in his sleep.

"What happened to you mate, you get frightened or something?"

"No, I waited up top a minute or two just in case he broke back up across the road like that other one. Then I thought maybe you might be scared and came down to save you. But I see you've learned what to do at last, Good on you mate, you'll make the grade yet."

"Yeah, I'm learning okay. But still don't know how to gut and carry them things. Can you teach me just once more?"

Keeping up the charade I replied "Sure mate. Nothing to it really. Watch me."

And within five minutes it was on my back and being toted slowly up the hill on our right, Sam opening up the dense underbrush for me and breaking off head-high branches and vines.

We were warm again and making good progress, only Rebel languishing in our rear. He had been worked over a bit by the pig and sported half a dozen small cuts and gashes. Shiney had a small poke under her chin, and looking at the pig's tusks, (not as long as at first supposed but incredibly sharp and dangerous), decided we were lucky to get away as cheaply as we did. Rebel probably paid too in that he was already tired before he started wrastling the pig and had no doubt been just fractionally slower then he otherwise would have been.

We changed over half-way down to the gorse track, it was Sam's turn and as we broke out of the tall gum trees couldn't help but notice the clouds were lowering and thickening not far above our heads. The day seemed darker, more sombre somehow and we hurried as best we could for the creek and the last haul up to the vehicles. Rain wasn't too far away and we were baulked at the creek, now swirling from the earlier rain and we had to leap for our lives to get across unburdened by the pig, leaving it tied to a long string to be hauled across last of all. It was wet now of course but we didn't muck about as we could see rain, up at the gum trees, coming down-valley like a solid wall and I hefted the pig forthwith and hoofed it for the truck. Half way we changed again and I carried the rifle while Sam took our 120lb boar the last few yards. We just made it too, shucked off the pig onto the deck and "booted" it for home.

The Unlucky Lucky Boar

There is a place I hunt from time to time a good way from here, which doesn't get a lot of pressure. It's pig population isn't great either and parts of it are about the hardest sort of cover to get through I've ever encountered. In places a tall form of swamp wi-wi is so dense and the growth so prolific the only way to make progress is to walk backwards, pushing your feet out behind you to gain another half metre. And when this rubbish is beaten you're immediately into similar stuff but of a longer, thinner variety, almost as hard to negotiate. In some of the places there I reckon it would be nigh impossible to approach a bailed pig – and that's if it could be bailed in the first place.

In parts too it was reasonably open pine forest, easy enough to get through, but it boundaried onto all that other horrible muck. And on another side it was bordered by farmland where grass, manuka and particularly gorse competed for dominance. In many places the gorse had won but Eddie and I had caught one or two good pigs there regardless. I had done quite a bit of hunting in the pines and on the gorse covered gentle rolling country of the farm but always hankered to have a real close look further out. According to what Eddie reckoned, that's where the bigger boars lurked, coming from time to time closer in and running foul of myself or Kelly Garton or some other itinerant hunter. Before getting to the other side of the block I had to cross a tidal creek and on the two occasions that I had ventured over that way, had had to go a long way upriver to where the tidal flow stopped, where two creeks converged near a steep face above the salt water. There was a pig track, or pig road more like, well travelled and on this there were marks of a heavy male pig heading both ways. That he used this particular track suggested to me that he lived out in all that hard country towards the peninsula. This was his most likely route to and from his den, indeed his most direct route to the pines and the farmland. At one stage I saw a really big hoof print in soft earth near the creek and guessed it might be the monstrous dog-killer Eddie and Richard Lawrence talked about from time to time. I decided it was time I had a go at running a hog or two to earth out that-a-way.

It didn't appear to be a very promising sort of day as I let the four dogs off their chains. I wasn't starting too early as I wanted to drop my chainsaw off at Greg's on the way past and he didn't open until 8'oclock. And as I topped the rise at Coopers Beach, rain spattered the windscreen, only briefly and not too heavily, but ragged thunderclouds were coalescing over the distant hills to the northwest. The air was cooling rapidly from what it had been and it looked altogether not good to be outside in another hour or so. The sun behind me shone bravely for another half an hour but was soon overtaken by a scrim of dirty clouds running ahead of the thunderheads moiling ominously over the water. I thought of valour, discretion, determination, dilly-dallying – and turned tail for home. Even as I pulled into home the rain became heavier and I had to put my jacket over my shoulders as I called the hunters to their chains and they were as disappointed as I was I'm sure, but it would only be seven more days and seven more sleeps till we tried again.

An hour later I was pleased I'd decided to cancel as rain and wind pummelled the house unmercifully. Water ran in little rivulets everywhere, the rivers were up later in the day and the met' service warned of heavy rain coming tonight and I was pleased I had the good sense to turn around when I did. Trouble was I got talking to Sam Harris in Whangarei who told me of a good boar he and Des had chased last weekend.

"You know the reserve where we looked for that pig a month ago, me and Des went back there last weekend with Prince, Joe and Jess. Des took Jess up the middle ridge and about half way up she bolted over the edge and started bailing on the far side of the basin. There's a lot of fern there eh, and she couldn't keep it in one place. Me, Joe and Prince heard her all right but we were one ridge over and by the time they got there the pig had broken and gone over into McKenzie's. Poor old Jess was ripped about and chucked it in even before Prince and Joe appeared and we never saw the thing again. Till today that is."

"Eh? Come again?"

"We caught it today," laughing now.

"Well, come on, tell me all about it you big skite," I said.

"There's not much to tell really. Des had seen some big marks on

Thursday where we caught that 100 pounder last year with whats'-'is
-name. Prince found him well down that steep face and him and Joe
chased him all right – right back in a big circle to us and we shot him as
he crossed the grass ridge between the nikau bush and Boyd's place. But
I reckon the dogs would have got him in the next gully. They were right
on his hammer and he looked pretty stuffed as he crossed the ridge. I
don't know why be climbed all that way back up. He could have gone
straight away to the quarry and the goat country – but we don't mind.
Des just had time to line him up when we heard the fence below the
totara twang.

"You lucky dogs," I was quite envious – had even thought of heading
Sam's way before deciding on Eddie's scrub. "Wasn't it wet, raining?"

"Not much, is now though, coming down in buckets!"

"Hey, how heavy d'you reckon. You weighed it yet?"

"What, the rain or the pig?"

"The pig you twit, the pig."

"Oh yeah! A bit disappointing really. The hooks aren't too bad but it
only went 148 on the scales. Looked a lot bigger crossing the ridge."

As you can imagine I was all fired up by the next weekend. Couldn't
have them Whangarei jokers beating me. I'll show them!

So on Saturday I got away well before daybreak with four dogs and all
the paraphernalia attributable to pig hunting. The range of hills where
we were going to find our quarry was dark and shadowy in the distance.
The dark land mass, rugged, strung out on the horizon, was yet some
kilometres away and I had the accelerator hard down, thinking I might
catch some vestige of scent on the damp grass if I was early enough.
As the twilight of dawn left, an amber-coloured sun peeped over the
eastern foothills and set about transforming the whole land, until half
an hour later no sign of the night remained. Away out to the west maybe
a slight shadow, not quite as light as the rest lingered to brush the distant
perimeter of the sky. Birds were on the move too, gulls winging out to
sea, and a bunch of turkeys fighting and gobbling in a paddock as I sped
past. A long line of sheep followed one another as they snaked over the
grass looking for greener morsels on the other side of – the confounded
fence was still there – and the gate was shut. I wondered if they'd turn
around and saunter back or just get the sulks and stand around hoping
for a miracle. I wouldn't mind one myself actually – and it could well be
one if I came home with a good pig on the back.

It was fully day when I parked the L200 Mitsi 'neath the pines, damp still underfoot, and here in the confines of the forest, but it wouldn't last more than another couple of hours at the most. Most of the scent would be gone with the increasing heat of the day and seeing that I still had a long way to go, didn't hang about.

Rebel wasn't all that keen to head on out as he usually did and hung back all the way through the pines. Tahi and Shiney were their usual selves though and scouted around very satisfactorily. I had never got onto pigs just here, though Eddie did show me a big boar's marks at the first small trickle we usually crossed, the first time we went walkabout out this way. He couldn't come today, he and his brother-in-law Jamie had some important work to do in the orchard so I was by myself. Me and my four dogs that is. Bud, ever my buddy, generally stayed close too, but was probably the most aggressive dog I had once a pig was discovered. But that part of it, those days, was generally the charge of his three kennel mates. Later in life he took to finding remarkably well himself, though not at any great distance.

Uphill, down dale, uphill and along, sidling until I hit the fence and cut across the triangle before me, crossing two main gullies overgrown by manuka, mingi-mingi and gorse and hit the pines again not far from the beehives which were usually there.

A brief flurry of excitement to start the day off occurred about five minutes below the first fence. All the dogs had gone out to my left and there wasn't much in the way of action. There were a few cow pats overturned reasonably freshly and I surmised it was just enough to remind the hunters of what they were about. It wouldn't hurt for them to have a good scout around as a warm-up, do them good actually. I kept going, gun over my shoulder, and gazing over towards the pine plantation. Next thing, I heard a pig blow, only forty metres away, then blow again – a big blow – a boar!

I stopped, swung the rifle to the ready, and heard some smashing of ti-tree, then nothing more. Rebel, I saw two minutes later, was nose down and heading away fast to the pines. Then Shiney and Tahi appeared on his trail and Bud turned up back with me. I was certain that those three dogs hadn't spooked the boar, or even known he was there. I must have alerted the thing, maybe Buddy had. But anyway, he was gone and my three dogs I reckoned were tracking another. No time was wasted now and I hot-footed it across that triangle of country, and 15 minutes later found me just inside the pines and listening hard.

Nothing was forthcoming and I decided to head for the tidal creek and that pig road around the toe of the steep spur. Hopefully I'd pick up the dogs there (or their scent – Buddy would let me know). Maybe I'd even come across the fresh marks of the pig that had so recently and obviously disliked my company.

Half way there Rebel and Tahi caught me up from behind, only five minutes ahead of Shiney who came from the same direction. Aha! It looked like the pig they had been scenting had gone left more, towards Whangatupere. I'd look at the scrub that-a-way on the way back maybe – if I got nothing where I was going.

Stopping for a spell to let the dogs recover somewhat I lay down on the pine needles that carpeted the floor of the forest, looked at my watch and thought I could spare fifteen minutes. I got to wondering what Sam and Des were up to, probably up towards Tutamoe and homing in on Joe's or Kiwi's voice and a big boar. I jumped up immediately and set off again – only three minutes respite had been sufficient to remind me I had to beat them to it today!

No sooner had I started off than all four dogs ran quickly back where they had come from and scored a 50lb boar apparently heading somewhere. Being on the scene fairly smartly allowed me to give the little pig his freedom and see him scamper off not badly harmed at all. He would be a much bigger and better opponent given a couple of years, not that I'd know him, he was all black with two ears and four legs. Pretty run-of-the-mill.

I had had to tie the pig up, then Tahi and Bud (I could call Shiney and Rebel off) and then, keeping a good eye on the first two, untie the little fellow and let him go. Now we waited about ten minutes and did have a good rest, Tahi and Bud ungracious at the pig's release, were now quite content to lie down still tied up and have a blow themselves.

It wasn't far from there really to the pig road I knew of and as I crossed the first small creek, saw immediately where a large member of the "porcus – swinus" family had very recently come this way too. His heavy indentations were rather obvious and the dogs had gone again, noses down and soon I was by myself.

Where the face was steepest, I didn't want to meet any great hairy wild pig head on and pushed on hurriedly, not worrying about making a noise and finally, crossing the second stream, could climb up onto a wee bit more level ground and crossed another small trickle, and then I was into big gorse and bracken. I battled my way straight ahead for an age it seemed with still no news of the dogs and came finally into a stand of manuka about three to four metres tall and very open underneath. This was really good and I headed uphill trying to follow the centre of the broad ridge having to veer one way and another and came at length to where it petered out and the thin - stemmed wi-wi took over. Now I slowed right down as there was a lot of smaller manuka about two and a half metres tall, a lot of it dead and dying, and this had fallen every-which-way. It meant I had to find a pig run and stick to it, breaking crossing manuka stakes all the time.

I was making quite a lot of noise as I hurried uphill trying to locate the dogs, or at least hear them off in the distance. There was no need to worry about the noise though for at that instant they all opened up fifty metres ahead. World War III had erupted a short distance beyond where I was, and the first thing I did was get my rifle ready for instant action. Gingerly now I crept forward still having to snap ti-tree stems all the time, (it wasn't at all possible to avoid doing so), and I knew the pig, boar that is, (because of the loud clamorous barking) knew I was coming. There was nothing anywhere near big enough to shinny up, the ground was gentle rolling and I was in the middle of a pig run with absolutely nothing to hide behind that would be of any use whatsoever.

But I had four dogs and three bullets! Rebel and Bud were doing a remarkable rendition of pig dogs at the bail. Persistent, in-your-face, no let up, "I dare you to try" noise many decibels beyond what I normally heard. Shiney and Tahi saw me and broke off to come, wagging their tails. "Soo! Soo! Get "im!"

Back they went, but I knew the boar was watching. I inched nearer, and at last saw the beast's flank with Rebel out front and Tahi to one side of him.

'Boom!"

Silence. Profound silence. Then vicious bailing again fifty metres uptrack. I'm sure I heard a solid thwack as the bullet struck it's side and I was confident we had him. Cranking my second bullet (I only had three) into the chamber, I let the hammer halfway down but kept my thumb on it and closed the gap again. This time I made no attempt to do so quietly but slowly pushed and snapped my way ahead to where they were confronting the beast.

The "click-clack" of tusks being honed was nerve-rattling and very real. He was only eight-to-ten metres away but slightly back-on this time and Shiney and Tahi did their "Greetings Boss" thing again (I could have shot the useless mongrels). But they went back and contributed

176

to the shindig again. The black thing moved and I could see Bud out beyond and Rebel showed momentarily between more wi-wis on the left. I waited. Bud came around to bail in slightly more open going along on the right almost behind the boar who was now facing Rebel. Next instant things became very lively. Tahi shot in and had a snatch at Mr Boar's jewels, he in turn spun and charged Tahi who had leapt backwards the same moment. Fortunately the open ground allowed Tahi the chance to scarper and Rebel feinted in turn, nipped the pig and retreated likewise. I only saw flashes of this but was ready and planted a second .44 bullet in the pig's abdomen (I thought).

This time the silence extended to about what seemed five minutes but can only have been less than one as I heard the dogs pull the boar a third time one hundred metres away in much the same sort of cover. He was climbing though and heading for a stand of pampas not too far off and I guessed one or two more breaks like previously and he would be in a pretty impregnable place.

I now had only one bullet left and confidently approached in short manuka and wi-wi. I could see all four dogs quite plain and Mr Pig had to be under those three big wi-wi bushes just there. All I had to do was wait till he succumbed from his wounds and I'd have him. But time went on, the dogs were getting blasé and the boar was continuing to clack his ivories every ten seconds, and I couldn't see him.

This stand-off went on and on. I couldn't get the dogs to attack and I was getting frustrated. As it turned out, neither of my bullets had found their mark and seeing I hadn't bitten his bum, he wasn't too worried about me so it seemed.

After half an hour all went quiet quite suddenly. The "click-clack" and growling of the pig stopped, the dogs hadn't barked for a half minute and I heard the pig go "Hmmm" and creep away. I heard him all right. I even saw the wi-wis shake but couldn't see anything I could shoot at. Besides, I was worried that I had wounded him and if he came back at me I'd have nowhere to go, no last bullet, disinterested dogs and I'm darn sure he wouldn't have listened to my protestations of peace and goodwill!

Rebel, Tahi, Shiney and Bud had had enough and were calling it a day. Peer as I might I hadn't been able to get another glimpse of anything resembling "Pig" and being anxious of the outcome of a bullet sent at a "venture" – thought again of valour, discretion, determination and dilly-dallying – and for the second time turned tail and set sail for home. I kept a "weather-ear" open behind me too you can be sure and was rather pleased to have four brave pig dogs in close proximity.

I called and had a yarn with Eddie as I left and told him to make sure he explained to Kelly Garton exactly where he might pick up a wounded boar tomorrow. For I knew Kelly was going to be hunting that same area and it would be a shame not to benefit from my bad luck (or useless dogs/markmanship or whatever).

Kelly did go the next day. It was wet and blustery but he and Peter Ru weren't to be put off by a tad of inclement weather. Eddie told Kelly about the pig I had had bailed up and certainly added to his enthusiasm but he and Peter were headed that way in any case as it turned out. To know there definitely was a big pig in the offing simply made it that much more exciting and them all the keener – if that were possible.

At this time Kelly had three really capable dogs, two holders and a finder-bailer. The two heavier dogs could find as well and sometimes were first to do so, though today was to be Nig's day.

Peter Ru was ready and waiting as Kelly stopped to pick him up at the cattle yards. Some time previously Eddie and I had dropped off a little boar, broken-coloured I seem to remember, and we had had quite a job deciding where to put him as the bottom rails of the yards were too high off the ground. Bits and pieces were poked in here and there and little piggy had a new home. I was a little sceptical about the likelihood of there being a pig still there the next day, but Eddie assures me it never did get away.

So, Peter was ready, had been since 6 o'clock, and waiting too, while Kelly was ready and driving.

Motoring up the forest road was certainly very much quicker and easier than my usual route and in no time Peter and Kelly were well up the hill, coming around to the right, passing a couple of side roads and slowly descending again to where the side track headed to the tidal creek Not far from the beehives the road divided, straight ahead being the way to Whangatupere, so Kelly swung his vehicle right, onto the track that wound in and out of the pines a considerable distance.

"I reckon we should leave the truck here Kelly, you never know, there might be a pig between here and the creek." Peter knew the area pretty well from past experience and voiced his opinion as they rounded the first couple of corners.

"Yep! Righto mate," Kelly returned. "Anywhere here?"

"Yeah. Yeah, anywhere will do."

They pulled over and between a row of well-grown larger trees running obliquely from the road. As they opened the doors they were greeted by a shower of raindrops from the disturbed branches overhead.

"Ugh! Cursed rain!"

"You can stay here if you like Peter, at least you won't melt."

"That'll be the day. I'm tougher than you mate, only I don't like having to prove I'm tougher, we both know it though eh!"

"Yeah, right!"

Nig and his two larger mates Hilo and Beulah wasted no time and hared off down the track and were out of sight pretty well straight away.

The two men looked at each other and smartly headed seawards too. The wind in the pines wouldn't allow much hearing to be done unless close to a punch-up so they made an effort to keep up with the dogs. At the far end of the first straight they saw Hilo just disappearing around the far corner and stepped on the gas. The end wasn't more than another half kilometre but a lot could happen in that distance they knew. Blustery squalls came out of the north as they finally hit more open going and the rain, not really what you could call showers, was nonetheless cold and frequent enough to put the damper on what ought to be a fine outing. Yesterday's fine weather was a thing of memory only, it was the "here and now" that mattered.

The "there and now" was to be far more exciting though. Kelly and Peter had only just crossed the head of the tidal part, heading roughly where my pig road led. The three dogs had taken straight to water and swam flat-out for the far side. While this was only seventy-odd metres, it meant a long haul round the head of the estuary because of the tide being in and too deep to wade.

As they got to about where I had hit that bigger gorse yesterday there was still no sign of Nig, Beulah and Hilo and Kelly was secretly all hyped-up and expectant. You could almost feel the tension. Peter, mouth open and head thrust forward stopped too and strained to listen!

"I wonder – "Kelly."

"Shh."

"D'you think-"

"Shh."

Peter had his hand up now, and even though Kelly had whispered, wasn't sure what, or if he had heard – something.

He began nodding his head as all hell broke loose not over one hundred metres beyond them. What he had heard was a pig blow and

Peter Greenhill, with a big black boar.

scrub rustling – he thought. But with the eruption of hostilities not far off he knew he had been right and grinned at Kelly. But Kelly wasn't there. He had moved and was still moving straight towards the action. The noise was pretty horrendous now, not too much barking except by Nig, but scoffing and crashing and the snapping of manuka stems. Then that dreaded "sound", the lack thereof had them pull up just metres short of where the battle had been joined. And moments later started again back behind them. The cunning pig had headed to a huge stand of pampas and bailed in the thickest of thickets he could find. There was a lot more barking now as he competently stood the three dogs off. This was his place, he felt comfortable here, safer than in the ti-tree and confidently faced his three attackers.

And he may have stayed there except for the one thing he hadn't experienced too much before. That horrible man-smell was getting close again. Yesterday had been bad enough. Now there were two of them and he panicked. Out he shot, Nig after him, and doing a couple of circuits in the cutty-grass opted to go downhill. It's generally a sign of being hammered (a boar, a wee way ahead of dogs more often tends to go up and over) and Kelly was guessing Hilo and Beulah must have been right there with Nig this time round. He and Peter literally flew downslope now, anxious to be there to help the three dogs should he bail again. And he did, not far above the water he decided to have it out once and for all. Backing up to an earthen bank he faced them. His nuts, already tender from Nig's ministrations were less vulnerable there he thought. Not so! Hilo, even more gutsful than discretionary just came at him. His mate, from a good many such encounters flew in a thousandth of a split-second later and there he was when Kelly hove into view. He had moved out in his endeavour to attack the two ear dogs and exposed his rear again. Nig darted in and grabbed him where it already hurt and so he sat down on the spot (on Nig's head as well).

Calling Nig off, Kelly had his gun up and just as the boar sensed victory in throwing the other two off, and charging away, let strip with his .30-30.

"Yeeha. You got him, Yoohoo!" This was Peter, usually a much more reserved sort of character I would have thought, but here he was as excited as Kelly and letting off steam in grand style.

"Yeah, we done it mate." Kelly slipped down the bank and pulled the boar onto his back to bleed him and inspect the tusks and general condition of their prey. "One good one and one broken one. Too bad. He's in good nick though eh Pete. Do you want him for your hangi on Tuesday?"

"Yeah! Too right. We can tow him most of the way and leave him at the landing. We might have to get our feet wet but that way we can keep clean and bring the ute right to it. Save a lot of carrying."

So that's what they did. Their 160-180lb black boar with mediocre tusks became hangi-fare and the thrill of the chase, the culmination of the fight and the excitement of it all more than compensated for the wet uncomfortable feeling that set in afterwards.

There were no bullet holes anywhere either. I must be as useless as my dogs!! And the poor old pig, he would have been all of five years old, had been lucky yesterday with Reg, not so lucky today with Peter and Kelly.

The Chopper Chopper

Many long years ago, I was working for my cousin Jim Tolmie, milking cows at Taratara Road in the far north. It was in the days when we separated the cream from the milk and fed the skimmed milk to a mob of pigs in the piggery. We had an old large-white boar who was at the end of his "use by" date and had to be mounted on rubber (put on a lorry for "the works"). But he had to be castrated first.

However were we going to get the cantankerous old boar to lie down while we did the necessary? We hadn't a clue.

But Wincey did! He was the local Pig Marketing Association (PMA) agent and readily agreed to perform said operation on Mr. Pig.

So on Tuesday morning Wincey Dangen turned up with his very super-duper sharp pocket-knife and a length of rope.

"Come and give us a hand Reg," he suggested. I looked at the rope, then at the size of the pig and decided I'd lend encouragement from a good distance away. On a few occasions I had helped de-nut weaners, holding them on their back between my boots, back legs pulled well forward and in no time it was over. But boy-oh-boy, did they squeal!

This huge animal was ten times their size and then some, and I reckoned once he got a lungful there'd be no stopping him. I can tell you I was apprehensive to some considerable degree, but Wincey went about the whole thing with aplomb. I did notice though, he didn't say anything of what we were planning to the daddy pig – and kept his pocket-knife hidden. This fellow had big teeth sticking out of his jaw, dangerous looking they were. Wincey was obviously minus a few teeth and looked like a pirate – dangerous too when that pocket-knife was in hand – leastways for the pig he was.

From the doorway, (which I kept open) I watched as Wincey made a loop in one end of his string, eyeing a reinforcing rod sticking out of the top of the concrete nib-wall. He had Jim bring some pig pellets and pretend he was doing Mr. Pig a big favour by tipping them out alongside this same low wall.

"When I've got him Jim, you come and hang onto the rope and I'll hop in the pen and do the trick eh? Shouldn't be too hard." Wincey was as nonchalant as you like (foolhardy I suspected) and set about fashioning a loop to drop, or manoeuvre over the boar's snout.

All went well for a minute or so. Every time the pig opened his jaw to gather up more pellets, Wincey tried to get that noose in his mouth behind his grinders – and eventually did. Then pandemonium broke loose. Wincey was yelling at Jim, Jim was yelling at me, I was yelling at anybody "What? Where? Eh?" And the pig was grunting and chomping and pulling as hard as he could backwards on that rope.

But Wincey had wrapped it around the reinforcing rod a few times and was pulling like crazy himself, anxious to trade places with Jim who was coming to the rescue very cautiously.

"Come on man, grab this rope here and hang on for all you're worth. Don't let him go or we'll never get it on him again. Got him? You sure? Good – good!"

In no time flat Wincey was in the pen behind the boar with his pocket-knife out, and squatting down for all the world like a parlour-maid milking her cow, he proceeded to relieve Mr. Boar of two stone(s). Mr. Boar wasn't at all impressed and (almost) literally lifted the roof off with the most horrendous squealing I'd ever heard. It only took a couple of swift sure slashes, a bit of a tug, another sideways stroke of the scalpel and it was done.

"You can let that rope go now Jim," he said grinning like a schoolboy as he held two large testicles aloft and hopped out of the sty. "Why don't you get Lois to fry these up for your's and Reg's lunch. Believe me, they've got a taste all of their own. Waste not, want not you know."

Jim and I thanked him profusely and took the big fat sausage-like things from him as he got in his car to head off. "That chopper will be ready to send off in a couple of weeks you men. He'll have healed up good by then, see you."

We watched him drive off, and when the dust was 200 metres away Jim tossed the dog his breakfast, which I think he enjoyed. We had to make do with porridge and scones.

That was how I found out that big boars, going to "the works" were referred to as "choppers". Sixty to eighty pound pigs were porkers, others around 130/140lbs were baconers, and now we had a chopper. You learn something every day!

Peter Greenhill's 220lb boar. A real chopper.

Years later, around early May 2006 Ricky and Gail Smith were up our way on holiday from the Bay of Plenty, and after hours and hours of talking I asked him: "Plenty of pigs back of your farm Ricky?"

"A few, not many. I'm going where there are a few though when I get back. Why don't you come and be my mate. I've got no one else jacked-up yet."

"Where're you going?"

"The Ureweras. Flying in by chopper next Monday. It'll only cost about $300 each. You'll really enjoy it man!"

Sure it sounded intriguing. And when Olive encouraged me to go I took the bull by the horns and said: "Yep, I'm in!"

Now I'd never been in a helicopter before and was a mite concerned re safety, height above ground, mechanical failure, pilot proficiency etc, etc, but reasoned that if Ricky wasn't scared, there was no way I was going to be. (And even if I was, there was no way he was going to know about it.)

Olive and I drove down to Te Puke and stayed with Gail and Ricky a while later, now the month of May, and a great deal of time was taken up with packing gears, deciding what not to take, what dogs were "in", and who had to stay home. This was an all new adventure for me. All my hunting of pigs up till now had been "one-dayers", except those yearly trips with Peter Greenhill and Alphonso Heihei to Te Paki. This in reality was very much like that. Apart from the fact that here we were miles in the bush and reliant on the pilot to return in four day's time. Which meant that if you needed something you had forgotten, you went without.

Monday started dark and crisp. An hour and a half before dawn we had risen, snaffled a quick breakfast and took off (once the dogs were loaded), for Murupara and the helicopter base.

We had had to wait three quarters of an hour as another lot of hunters and dogs were scheduled ahead of us and were heading in to the Boyce hut. Didn't mean a thing to me but Ricky knew where they were heading.

"Is that anywhere near where we're going Ricky?"

"Yeah – nah, well not really, sort of, kinda."

"We likely to bump into them in the bush?"

"Yeah – nah. I don't reckon."

I sort of, kinda deduced we'd probably be lucky to see them, more than likely, maybe.

In no time at all the wonderful flying machine was beating it's way back from yon far horizon and became a helicopter instead of a speck in the sky, eventually thrashing air down at us as it came in to land on the concrete pad for our turn. Now I was all excited (and nervous at the same time). I was all agog watching Ricky and Snow weighing gear, estimating dog tonnage, counting packages etc, (paying money) and then cramming it all in that small vibrating machine. At last we got the dogs aboard and went to climb in ourselves.

"You can have the front seat seeing it's your first time if you like Reg," offered Ricky magnanimously. "You'll be able to see the countryside far better than being perched in the back like me."

"Gee, thanks mate."

There wasn't much room left for our parachutes I thought, and was wondering when they were going to be produced when Snow came around my side, slammed my door, climbed in the pilot's seat and revved up. "Uh-oh" my stomach said, no parachute. I glanced hurriedly round at Ricky and was just going to ask when the thing did a wobble and jumped up off the concrete.

"Wheeee" – we were up and off.

"You okay mate?" asked Ricky. "Not scared at all?"

"Yeah, nah." (what a stupid question!) My guts were a trifle, well, slightly anxious – no, more like concerned perhaps, just a little. But the real me was right as rain mate, right as rain.

Actually it was, well, sort of – neat, in a squeaky sort of way. We were some 100 metres (I guessed) above the ground and ascending the slope of a fairly high ridge of grass and scattered scrub. If we crashed now it was just vaguely possible we'd make it, I think. Then we got to the crest of the hill and we were "omigosh", fair leaping skywards, the ground dropping away at a thousand miles an hour. Now we were way up in the wild blue yonder, that tiny speck again, and houses and horses and hills were just little wee things way below. Cor! If it happened now we'd be "goners". Best to just keep your eyes on the horizon Reg. Can't be too far for us to go, another five minutes maybe.

Suddenly, the horizon lurched, wobbled a bit and steadied again. After my heart settled I glanced at Snow, who was all this time chatting away quite unconcernedly with Ricky in the back about previous flights in and out that they had done together. I tried to think of some intelligent question to ask my "mate" Snow, but nothing seemed to come.

I wondered if Ricky would be quite so calm if he could see out like me. I'd bet he wouldn't be quite so cool and collected if he knew how high we were. The stupid little aluminium thing we were in lurched again and I was nearly going to help the pilot with that joystick thing if he needed it, but he wasn't at all phased by it, it would seem. A bit of "turbulence", I found out later. (I wish someone had explained all this before we started).

"Where we headed Snow?" (now that sounded nonchalant didn't it ?)

"See that gap in the far hills? There's a gorge cutting in behind there where that cloud is rolling in – somewhere in there."

"How long?" (my voice wasn't squeaky that time).

"'Bout fifteen minutes."

That was miles away, and not getting noticeably closer – yes it was – minutely – just.

We were flying over thousands of acres of native forest now. Just bush and bush and gullies and steep ridges and rivers, rocky outcrops, jagged sawtooth tops with no safe flat land for hundreds of miles. Everywhere was dark green, tree green, shades of green and more hills and gullies than ever you could imagine. Wild and beautiful it was, awe inspiring in it's immensity and ruggedness and we were going to crash in the middle of it!

186

I prayed a lot. Quick short prayers especially when the flimsy thing lurched a little bit, or a big bit. "Lord, you said we could trust you. Well, right now I'm relying on you. Please keep me (and Ricky and Snow and Flash and Queenie and Brin and Jet) safe here. Please?"

The wonderful thing about God is His faithfulness – and I'm still here. (If ever this book gets published and I have to get a complimentary copy for Ricky I'm going to rip this page out. I don't mind him knowing I was praying, but he's not to know I was – you know – um, well, slightly concerned).

I was thinking of his and Snow's safety was all.

By the time we got to that gap in the hills I was an experienced and intrepid helicopter co-pilot and totally at ease.

"Have a gander at Hugo's 'palace' Snow. See if it's still standing after that storm a month ago," Ricky suggested now.

"Was going to anyway, nearly there. It's in that next gut ahead. A flat place – you'll see it."

They did. All I caught was a brief glimpse of something and shut my eyes – very tight! Snow had banked the chopper in a real tight turn above this gut and I was sitting on the lefthand door. Below me, moving sluggishly away there was a hut I gather–and we were going to fall on it, I knew! We were at stalling speed and ready to drop out of the sky. The whirling thing above us – I mean beside us was making a funny "shop – shop" sort of noise and sounded as worried as I was.

Somehow we survived and levelled out again. The day of miracles is not past, praise the Lord! I unclenched my teeth and started to relax and breathe again. Flying now up a side-stream to the main river we had been following, I was ogling the magnificent scenery below. It was beautiful native bush with undulations everywhere – gullies and spurs and "flattish" places all festooned with greenery of every imaginable shade was spread out below us.

Then we really lost it! She started coming down. Or the land was coming up extremely fast. I could see out of the corner of my eye Snow wrestling frantically with the levers and things he used to fly with, but we were now in free-fall, somehow staying fantastically level. I hung on and prayed again, very quickly and with eyes shut tight. Solid looking trees were rushing up to spear us from underneath and I pulled up my knees and got ready. The crash when it came was surprisingly gentle, we were still right way up, and would you believe it, intact. We must have got really, really, really "lucky". Of all the thousands of acres we'd flown over we'd managed to hit the dirt in the only tiny area in all that immensity, devoid of trees. A tiny wee clearing in the limitless jungle, and we had come down on it. Incredible! You just wouldn't read about it.

Snow was relieved we were in one piece I could tell and was yawning and stretching. The poor old chopper was winding down too. I stumbled out, fell on my knees and kissed the ground, (not). I just felt like it and Ricky would have laughed. I expected Snow to walk around inspecting and looking for damage, radioing for help, sending out a "mayday" or something. He simply came around my side, thumped me on the shoulder and said: "Wasn't too bad after all eh Reg," grinning from ear to ear. The penny was starting to drop. He had gone to help Ricky unload all our gear and dogs and didn't see my clasped hands and huge sigh of relief.

"See you in four days Ricky," he said, hopped back in the chopper and flew away. I was amazed, it could still fly! But I suppose, we didn't actually crash after all did we. I wasn't about to let on to Ricky by asking any stupid questions either. Interestingly enough, when we finally got home and were talking about how I had gotten a grandstand view while he was jammed in the back with packs and sleeping bags and tarpaulin etc packed all around him, he came out with: "Yeah, but if we'd crashed I'd have been cushioned by all that gear." (I felt a little bit better after that).

Ricky grinned now and nodded over his shoulder: "Camp's through there a wee way. We'd better hump our gear over and get settled before mid-day if we can. Maybe a chance for a hunt after lunch if we're lucky." And picking up a big duffel-bag type of thing and a rifle, ducked into an opening in the fringe of ponga behind him. I grabbed a load of boxes and stuff and set out to follow. Sure was different to where I usually hunt. Ferns and mosses, lichen and ponga, reeds and rata vine and trees of all sorts smothered the land with greens and browns, and after twisting and turning a dozen times and calling out once, I found my mate already pulling polythene over a ridgepole.

It took maybe an hour to set up camp. Ricky found things he had hidden on a previous trip, fire-starters, a machete, rubber matting and utensils, all stored in holes under a bank or in a split tree-trunk.

He told me to go down to the river for some water and very soon had a hot drink ready.

Dogs were tied handy and beds made ready, bags resorted and firewood gathered so that when we returned at day's end all would be ship-shape and ready for us to inhabit.

By 1pm we were keen for a foray into the jungle and got knives, gun, string and torches etc. all ready and let off the dogs. A minute later the first pig squealed up behind camp. Flash had homed in on that smell that had been tantalising him for the last half hour, and caught this seventy pound boar not too far past where the chopper had landed. Ricky boned it out and we were off downstream soon after.

Numerous small water-courses split the slope coming down from the main ridge far above us and in these damp places and other gullies shy of the sun, pig sign was plentiful. Yet for all the abundant evidence of swine it was at least two hours before we actually found one. Jet worked like a Trojan, investigating very thoroughly every piece of rooting we came across. I daresay the continual dampness and shade contributed to the appearance of little time having elapsed since the market-gardeners had been at work. Whereas, truth to tell, much of what we saw and took to be recent, may possibly have been a day or days old. All three finders, Flash, Jet and Brin were convinced pigs were in the offing, and even Queenie scouted around more than she normally does.

Another sixty-ponder "went west" to Jet's perseverance. Up a steep-sided ridge she had tracked, nose to ground, and we decided to follow smartly when Brin and Queenie returned and followed suit. It was fairly rugged climbing for the first 100 metres but levelled off onto a broad slowly ascending plateau-like football field. The ground dropped away smartly on either side to a boulder strewn hollow on the left and a dark, deep gully on the right. Up at the far end where the goalposts could have been Jet had cornered her medium-size pig, and again Ricky boned it out.

Home, or camp, was over an hour away so we turned back and retraced our steps down the Wairau River before turning up our creek. I was surprised at how open the forest was, having envisaged it more like Northland bush and much more dense. Probably the deer and possums and pigs kept it that way–which was good as far as travel was concerned, and for seeing far ahead. In places it was tighter admittedly, and you had to work at it, but not too often.

The sudden dip and "S" bend ahead told us we were only a few short metres from camp and we thankfully dropped what we were carrying a minute or so later. Ricky being main, chief, number one and only cook, got tea on while I tied the hunters up and gave them a feed. They were happy too no doubt to lie and munch on Tux biscuits and loll about;

certainly it seemed like it to watch their antics.

We were in bed not long after dark, listening to the moreporks of the surrounding area, and there were a few of them. Possums too called from various points and at one time after we had stopped yarning, we heard a peculiar noise, distant though, from away upstream towards Lake Waikaremoana.

Just what it was neither of us could imagine. A long diminishing wail in the distance was enough to make our hair stand on end and we listened for it again but it wasn't repeated. This was around "ninish" and we were perplexed by it a tad. Very definite in it's intensity, even though far off, and I thought of things like Yeti, moa, aliens or lost souls wandering the wilderness, something unknown and unrecognised.

Finally sleep came, for an hour or so at least, till we were awakened again in the middle of the night by raindrops that got heavier by the minute. Within a quarter hour it was bucketing down and we had been out checking the dogs, untying two so they could creep in under the tarpaulin and keep dry. I at last went back to sleep and woke in the morning to Ricky's "Get out if you can Reg, the whole blinkin roof's collapsed." I staggered out in my bare feet to find the water, having formed puddles in the hollows between guy-ropes had eventually sagged the roof so much that it was pretty well all on the ground.

It took us a good couple of hours to reinstate our temporary home away from home, and we were a bit shy on string when we were finished. However, with this new idea of boning out pork as we caught it, string for pig-carrying wasn't such a necessary item as it usually is for me.

Ricky had put the meat into sealable bags and I had immersed it all in a small trickle of water behind camp, the idea being to keep it cool for the chopper to carry out.

Day two saw us finally sorted again after the rain/camp fiasco and we got away around ten, hunting downstream and up the Wairau, covering a fair amount of territory again.

"Do you ever see deer Ricky, there seems to be a fair amount of droppings around?"

"Yeah – nah."

"Eh?"

"Yeah – there is a lot of the stuff on the ground all right. But nah, we don't see too many. Not here I mean. Across the side-stream opposite camp we've got one or two at times in the past. I wanted to go there today but the rain's put the rivers up. By tomorrow it'll be cool I reckon."

"You gonna have a try if the river's down a bit?"

"Depends. There's a big big waterfall downstream of where we cross and if it's too risky we'll flag it. I know of a chap who lost a dog over it – never saw it again."

With that sobering thought we carried on. Jet had been gone a long time now and the tracker wasn't picking her up. "We'll cross that main ridge's toe soon enough now Reg, she may be up there somewhere out of range."

A huge bend in the river, obviously in flood, allowed the ridge referred to to stick it's toe into the water a fair way to our left. Here supplejack had found a favoured place and grew in profusion everywhere we turned. Brin, Queenie and Flash negotiated it in fine style, whereas Ricky and I squirmed and twisted and fumed for about a half hour and climbed at last out of it onto the ridge where sunshine endeavoured to shine through.

I found a place where sunbeams were lighting up a small knoll and stood there basking in the unaccustomed warmth. The shafts dappled the forest floor for perhaps ten minutes before the clouds jealously gobbled them up again and all was gloom and shade once more.

Meantime Ricky had his tracker out and was looking very intently towards the river.

"Hear something Rick?"

"Vaguely."

"Which direction?"

He didn't answer me for a few moments, then said emphatically, "She's down at the river about at the toe of this ridge. I can just pick her up faintly – did you see which way the others went?"

I hadn't even been aware they had gone – too busy basking in the sunshine. Can only have gone moments ago though. If they had've been my dogs I'd have known precisely where and when they had vanished. But Ricky was doing that part of it so I had gotten lazy I guess.

"No, I didn't mate, they were here only seconds back. Oh, there's Queenie now – and Flash. Can't see Brin though."

"We'll wait a sec", then head down to Jet. I think she's crossed the river and is on the other side."

"Right."

Brin appeared from uphill, sauntering towards us – "no pigs about just here Boss."

Ricky didn't hang about then and ten minutes later saw us all at the water's edge. Swollen with all the recent rain she was a turgid, turbid, seething mass of water. Trees careered past, smaller ones bouncing on the waves, heavier ones lurching and plummeting through the billows, racing ever on to the sea. And there on the far side was Jet, and a drowned 100lb black pig, only just starting to edge out into the current. She hung back on the far bank wagging her tail but keeping abreast of her pig, watching it slowly being eddied out more into the turbulence a couple of metres from shore.

"You watch the dogs Reg, I'll hop across and get it, and Jet."

"Don't be daft man! You'll end up at Mohaka, look at them trees."

"It's normally only a half a metre deep here. I reckon."

"I reckon you're cracked. You get in there man, we'll never see you again. It's not worth it mate." "I nearly drowned doing that sort of thing once."

"Yeah – I s'pose so."

"What about your dog?"

"She got across, she'll get back. We'd better get cracking. By the time we get home it'll be well after dark."

"Lucky I brought my new wind-up torch then eh! At twenty dollars it'd better be good. I see you've got your head-lamp as well, that's a LED light too isn't it?"

"Yeah man, champion little thing and so easy to cart all day in your pocket."

Leaving Jet to her pig, which wasn't really her's any more (it had just reached the mainstream current and was off bobbing and ducking on it's way to the sharks) we started climbing the ridge to get around the side where it appeared too steep and rugged to traverse.

Four hours later we were back at our bivvy. The last two were slow going with light rain or drizzle and my torch's light-giving interval not being very long-lived. Constantly having to wind the thing up was a bore and Ricky ploughed doggedly on.

"I feel we're close now Reg," was something I heard that often I didn't even listen to it any more. I think he was just trying to encourage me to keep up if I could. I made it, pretty tired and weary and was in my sleeping-bag rather soon. Not much talking was done that night.

The morrow was brilliantly and marvellously clear and we got away about 8:30am Ricky was keen to get across the side-stream if we could, and have a try for a deer if they were around. We could hear the river from camp and it didn't sound any less boisterous, but on arriving at the crossing- place it was definitely possible – said Ricky! The idea was to take two dogs each on a rope lest they be swept away downstream and over the waterfall we could plainly hear thundering and sending up spray not far away.

Ricky went first – and made it. He knew from past experience where to go and I followed soon after. Half way over, he hadn't told me, was a deep fissure in the streambed, and water roared through this gateway of rock, only a metre wide. But being up to my knees anyway in a very swift current, I didn't fancy our chances of hopping across this submerged chasm. If I didn't make it I was hoping the dogs would rescue me – but that was absurd, they were only touching bottom on an odd occasion and were practically swimming at the end of the rope I held.

And only forty metres below, just to add to my worries was where the water gushed foaming into a churning cauldron of a pool below a metre and a half drop. Not the big waterfall of another 100 metres further away – just a bit of a rapid he called it. I could see the rock shelf a metre away; it looked smooth and slippery and slanted slightly down-slope. No way there! Crabbing sideways left I found a somewhat wider portion of the hidden fissure, though with a two inch wide well-defined crack running away from me and heading towards the far bank. Ricky was yelling (I couldn't hear a thing) and pointing and gesticulating madly, both arms going flat out and I couldn't make out what he meant, up, down, sideways, backwards or whatever. I looked at the poor half swimming, half drowned dogs, took another turn of the string around my wrist, eyed that little crack in the rock and made a gigantic leap of faith. I stumbled and staggered a bit – but I had made it too, and soon was able to let the poor dogs ashore to get their breath back.

While I was elated, I was also now anxious re the return trip in a few hours. If the sky so much as darkened I was going to be off back to camp before any rain came. And having told Ricky as much I kept a weather eye on the sky all day. We walked and climbed a fair way, the bush being even more open on this side, and yet more still the higher we got. The wind was up a bit this morning yet it remained sunny, and even though we never got a run or a shot, enjoyed following the dogs. Several lots of largish pig rooting were come across but the perpetrator had seemingly moved on and out of range.

We badly wanted a good sized boar to show for our chopper money but it wasn't to be – not that side of the creek anyway. Then about 2pm we thought we'd better make a turn for home, and did so, veering left and descending almost to the water to work the riverbank all the way back to our "safe" crossing.

Ricky went first again, and again made it okay. It really encouraged me when I saw him slip nearly over at the halfway point, recover with a lot of arm-flailing and high-stepping and splash ashore to flop down recovering his breath.

Could I make it if I walked all the way to Waikaremoana and then out to Murupara? Yep, I could! Only, I'd probably get lost – take the wrong ridge etc. etc. So in I went. If Ricky could do it, I could do it better! Managed the fissure/chasm part okay, didn't nearly slip over, but then got cocky and released the two dogs too early and had them battling the current all by themselves. They made it though, but I didn't. I was dry all right, but got a growling from Ricky over releasing the dogs too far out.

"If you had gone over the waterfall, there's plenty more mates I could get to come next time," he said. "But if Queenie or Flash had gone over, I could never replace them, they're really valuable you know." This was my "mate" talking.

I took my medicine like a lamb. Being chastened as I was, I was a little subdued heading back to camp. The dogs weren't though. With only 100 metres to go they all shot uphill and Ricky and I looked at each other. Forgotten was the river crossing, the one way altercation, the wet boots, even the tiredness. Minutes passed before a long way above camp we heard barking, followed within seconds by a heavy squeal.

"Good pig Reg, come on!"

"Coming, you go."

And off he went like a rabbit. No effort was apparent in spite of our previous seven hour hiking and I envied him being as young as he is. I followed (I seem to do a lot of "following" these days) and homed in on the squeal, then the general noise as I got closer. He had already started gutting it when I arrived, and was going to bone-out the 80lb boar as soon as he had skinned it.

"I'll do that Ricky, if you like. You'd better follow your dogs. They've gone again, up past those nikau there."

A scented message had come wafting on the down-draught from the ridge way above and Brin, implacable when that odour was about was determined to track down it's originator. Flash followed with Queenie, scenting as they assailed the slope, adrenalin already enhancing their endeavour for they knew, all three, the battle looming only minutes away. Jet too was present, in the van with Brin, eyes searching as she toiled upwards.

The beginning of the afternoon gloaming was pervading the forest at this hour, but the hush would only last another short while. Intensity and earnestness accompanied them, and over-riding all was the exhilaration of impending battle. But to find him was a start, and the boss had better come!

"Oh, right," said Ricky at once. "I'll swap you knives though. This one's pretty sharp compared to your's. Your's will be good enough to stick anything with though."

We traded blades as suggested and I carried on. Ricky disappeared uphill and I never saw him again for about twenty minutes. Meantime, I had all the easy-to-get-at meat stashed in plastic bags and was about to head straight down to the hut when I heard a strange noise. Higher yet were alien sounds for in the bush. Noises not heard everyday, strange noises that didn't fit. There was a commotion going on a long way above me, and already I was running and climbing fast for I was pretty sure what it was. Only a biggish boar could solicit such an uproarious racket as assailed my ears. Could we be so lucky? Would Ricky arrive before me? Could the four dogs contain the thing till we were on hand?

A great rata stood on the centre of the ridge, and as I jigged past on the higher side, battle commenced in earnest above me. Though out of sight, all was clear to tell. The snorting and yapping, the crash of bodies and stomping of hooves, the smashing of branches and limbs and twigs all told me that Yeehay! we've got a boar!

Just over a small rise the steam was rising as I was closing in. Excitement's not the word here, it's something beyond that. Fear, exaltation and anxiety all wrapped up in exuberance and wanting were at the forefront just now and sweat ran down my face as I tried to beat Ricky there.

Fat chance! He was there ahead of me – just, but I never saw him. For at that moment the boar, the whole 140 approx. pounds of him was coming at me, or down upon me with no idea of giving way. I side-stepped and he missed me by half a millimetre, his ivories sweeping past and just missing my jeans as he hurtled by. His stench hit me like a rock wall at the same moment, sweet and sickly and powerful, not really nauseating – somehow the right smell, it just seemed to fit and conveyed memories of a thousand others before him. "Rocket Ricky" was on full blast too, and swept by in the wake of his dogs. I puttered in turn in HIS wake.

Brin had his measure though I could see. Even as he rocketed past this big brindle/black dog was almost part of him. Right at his bum, teeth were flashing and slashing and doing their deadly work.

Every endeavour was towards keeping pace, with enough left to harry that black bristly backside. And it worked.

Well out of sight they pulled him up again. On a downhill run all the way they had done extremely well. Flash and Brin never let up till finally, nearly half way back to camp, with one testicle on a tendril he decided enough was enough. Turning to do battle he was still too slow. Queenie was there as he turned and with a mouthful of pig's ear, hung out over the boar's snout momentarily. Flash grabbed his other one, and before he even thought to poke with his tusks, the girl-dog was back, helping anchor him to the spot, pulling hard to the rear along his flank. Jet and Brin sailed in with a will and did what they'd done umpteen times before. Working together the whole team, dogs and man overwhelmed their adversary today and conquered. And while it's not always so, sometimes it is, like now, and all were winding down as I arrived a few seconds later.

It was latish by this time and I offered to heft the boar back to our bivvy while Ricky tried to locate the earlier pig that I had put into plastic bags. He set off almost immediately and I gutted the big black pig, and struggled to my feet.

"Just keep to the ridge Reg for about a quarter of a kilometre, and where it flattens out more, turn left. You'll be practically above camp then. Hey, lay a trail as you go, just in case."

I was tired, pretty exhausted truth to tell, and by the time I had gone the quarter kilometre I had got to the towing stage. Part of the excuse was having to lay that trail for Ricky and therefore having to re-hoist the pig. I found I could drag the animal downhill for about 100 metres, turn back and leave silver-fern fronds upside-down to show even in the moonlight, or starlight (if any). Another 100 metre drag, another 100 metre trail of silver-ferns to lay – and so on.

I turned left where I thought I should and tugged and pulled into the falling gloom, broke off more fronds and did the same again. The boar weighed 200lbs by now and I was just a tad anxious. I knew I'd get home, though maybe I'd have to leave the pig till morning and just lay a trail so's I could find it again.

"Reg,–- Reg,–- AHOY!" At last!

"Down here Ricky."

He appeared a short time later and we had a spell for a little while.

"Found the other pig all right, after a bit of a search. Well, Flash did really. I was watching all the dogs all the time and he led me to it in the end."

"Great, where's the meat now?"

"Back at camp. I came looking for you straight away. By the way, you still got my knife?"

"Yeah – ah – (searching) – na. Must have left it where I gutted the thing. Sorry Ricky."

"S'okay, I'll get it." He glanced at his watch, looked all about and decided to go up and look for it right then. All he had to do was follow the silver-ferns (and they really showed up in the twilight) and with his head-lamp, ought to locate it easily enough.

"You're only about 80 metres above that little sharp ridge by the chopper pad, over there. See you soon."

He found his knife (thanks to the brilliant trail-laying), I found my way home with the boar, and we slept like logs.

In the morning with the chopper coming at 10am, all we had time for was to dismantle our bivvy, stow unspoilable gear in hiddy-holes and nooks and crannies etc., cart our baggage the wee way to the heliport and tie the dogs handy after getting the plastic bags of pork out of the creek.

I learned two things in a hurry that last hour we waited. One was probably something I may never have thought of till too late. That was, the necessity of actually tying the dogs handy to the landing-site, as otherwise they could well take fright at the incoming chopper and scatter.

The more important lesson was the result of finding all my bags of pork had gone "off". I'd never done it before, always hunting and going home the same day. At Te Paki we had access to a freezer; here I just cut and bagged. But when Ricky explained it to me it was obvious. I do actually remember him gutting and bagging his pigs, and he would always cut the meat off the frame and hang it on a branch for a while. I couldn't make out what he was up to. He thought, or supposed I knew.

Yeah, you've got it! The meat has to cool off! Mine was still warm when bagged and had no show of lasting even though it was submerged in the cold water of the creek. His was wind cooled, even up to half an hour, and tasted wonderful months afterwards. But I know now!

Bang on time the little speck in the sky became the chopper and it came in as gentle as you like to land almost on top of us. Now I was worried again. We would be carrying extra weight this time with our pork, and the rather solid-looking boar. Would we be able to lift off?

"Yeah, but we've eaten all that food we carried in don't forget," Ricky pointed out. "And the dogs are lighter and leaner too, we'll be okay!"

I was to ride shotgun again up front with Snow and we stashed all our gear in and on and around Ricky in the back seat. Dogs were stowed in the dog box, our boar was thrown in on top of Mr. Smith and we climbed in. Or another way of saying it is our boar, now a chopper, was put in the chopper, became in fact a chopper chopper and we were up, up and away.

Out The Back Door

Late in the winter of 2007 I had arranged with Sam Harris to go hunting on the Saturday in the scrub opposite where Ben's car had been laid to rest. We had chased a couple of good pigs a week before, a rank-smelling red boar of about 180lb plus, and a black one slightly smaller. The black one didn't strike me as being particularly smelly as it ran past twenty seconds after the bigger fellow and could perhaps have been a barrow. We were hoping to cut their sign again tomorrow, having some idea where they were headed.

Then on Friday Kalvin rang wanting to come too and I thought, seeing as how he hadn't met Sam it mightn't be a bad idea at that and we'd certainly have some good dogs on hand. Sam's dogs lately were being spectacularly successful, Joe and Kiwi doing everything right seemingly and I was hopeful these, along with mine would be able to successfully bail at least one of the two pigs referred to. Kalvin said he wouldn't bring his dogs as we'd probably have enough – sentiments I concurred with.

Saturday promised to be a lot more like spring really. The forecast was for a sunny day with moderate easterlies and a possibility of rain later in the afternoon, but we'd be finished by then.

Arriving early, I found Kalvin already there, not that that was a surprise. What was, was that he had brought his other hunting mate with five dogs as well and I immediately thought "three's company, four's a crowd." Not that I minded Brian coming – it was simply the timing. There would be far too many dogs now anyway so after "intros" were done, (after Sam turned up) I suggested a two-pronged attack. Not a pincer movement; we were going to assail the hill and split up at the top.

As it turned out, we split at the bottom, Brian and Kalvin heading along the bottom edge of the bush, and Sam and I hitting the scrub at the far corner of the sedge paddock.

They were to find the track which would take them to the top, then come back along the skyline to meet us at the bulldozed road near some gnarly old pine trees.

Sam and I fell into our usual routine. When down his way he led and I followed. When up my way, as now, I went in front and he tagged along behind. The dogs simply did their thing too, some fossicking about handy to us, others already lost in the gloom of the undergrowth. Pig-sign wasn't plentiful at all, and I was a little despondent thinking maybe we should have gone where Kalvin and Brian had. The gently ascending ridge we were on was a nursery area for wait-a-while and if you were to get off the track which I kept more or less open, it was highly likely there would be a seething mass of the prickly, clinging stuff – almost, but not quite, impossible to get through. I hated it and was somewhat relieved to arrive at the boundary fence running down through the manuka without having to charge off into the billowing, snarly tendrils of it. I usually called it "bush-lawyer", my mate Ray Murray from Tuatapere reckons it's "barrister" (it really gets it's hooks into you); and then one day I heard it referred to as this "wait-a-while", and to my way of thinking it seems pretty appropriate. On all the river faces this horrible stuff, mainly the small round-leafed variety, had established itself very convincingly – I avoided it where I could.

We ended up waiting a while near the boundary fence as we listened for the dogs to bark again. I thought I had heard one open up momentarily as we topped the rise. Not too far above now was the bulldozed road and we decided to head straight up to it just in case we had to cover distance in a hurry. But somehow I got lost, came back down the ridge, thought again, turned around once more and pushed through a plantation of pampas and stepped out into the arms of Kalvin and Brian. They had heard us floundering around below them like a herd of elephants they reckoned, and the barking I had heard was, one of our dogs barking at them as it burst out of the scrub.

"You must have given it a fright I guess. Probably thought you was a boar, or a smelly old billygoat." I wrinkled my nose frowning, and averted my face. It was only when I put my arm over my mouth that Kalvin caught on and began to laugh.

"Yeah, well, I'd rather be smelly than ugly like you. At least I can have a bath at Christmas, you'll never change."

I never took offence (he's bigger than me). And besides, everybody, but everybody knows I'm handsome. He was just trying to get even with me. We slung a bit more ridicule at each other and finally got around to discussing our next moves.

"Why don't you chaps tag along with us 'till we get to Williams' gate? Sam and I'll head up the steep ridge beside the pines and you chaps can meander down the old road. We'll be high and you'll be low and probably we'll catch something between us," I suggested.

"Aw thanks Reg." This from Brian. "We thought we'd like to head back and further along the ridge the other way and have a gander out towards the grass. There's a good mark on the track back that-a-way and we think he may be in those young pines. If that's okay with you?"

"Yeah sure Brian. You and Kalvin have a look. Whoever catches the biggest pig gets shouted an ice-cream by the losing team."

"You're on, I want a double hokey-pokey dipped in chocolate," laughed Kalvin.

"Ha! Fat chance."

"We'll show you." He was rapidly disappearing out of sight. Then after they were out of earshot I remarked to my mate, "That mark must have been bigger and fresher than they're letting on I reckon, eh Sam!"

"Yeah. I'm a bit suspicious myself. But come on, there's got to be a pig up there somewhere."

As it turned out, nobody got an ice-cream, or a pig. Sam and I had a good look right to the top of the airstrip hill, and nary a thing did we chase. Kalvin and Brian had already gone when we got back and Sam followed pronto himself. Jodi was expecting their first baby and he didn't want to be away longer than was truly necessary. I was disappointed for him having come all the way from Whangarei on a wild goose chase. (Never caught one of those either). But he's a pretty experienced hunter now and knows "them's the breaks".

But apparently Kalvin and Brian had had a bit of luck down their end of the scrubby block. He was pretty excited and rang me that same night. Well along the ridge, with younger pine trees on the left, and native scrub on the right, their dogs did indeed find a good boar and bailed it a few times well down near the raupo swamp below the plantation. They raced off but never quite made it and after the third bail had gone quiet were about to head back to the ridge when a big pig suddenly appeared, heading uphill too, all by itself. Having supposedly lost the dogs somewhere down near the water, it was making it's get-away, and came powering up the hill not too far below them. Seeing them pretty well on his escape route, he veered more left to pass them by, and was gone before much could be done about it. The dogs appeared eventually but never put up another bail the rest of the day. Maybe the boar was still in the vicinity – could Kalvin come out on Saturday with two or three dogs and try again? Brian wasn't going to be able to make it so it would be just him and me.

My youngest daughter Angela and her boy friend Mike were coming up from Whangarei and wanted to go for a walk over the river from where we were going to hunt. There was a good road through the bush, a really lovely place to stroll along, a place where pigeons visited regularly and tui were evident more often than not, where huge old puriri trees stood about, and twenty-two kauri graced the area among all the other trees of the forest. There were tanekaha, miro, kahikatea and taraire, a few rimu and of course all the lower storey of shrubs to wander through, and glow-worms in the dark under the eaves of the banks, a truly enchanted and romantic spot.

Well, I'd have to leave them to it. I had more exciting stuff to occupy myself with and met Kalvin just on day-break at the ford.

"We're gonna get a good one today Reg," was his first conversation piece.

This was another calm and sunny winter's day, cool at this time of the morning, invigorating perhaps, would be a better word. He had brought Brian's dogs for a run as Brian couldn't make it. Something about a bit of an accident and was hurting a little – could Kalvin give his dogs a run for him?

I had my usual team of Tahi, Shiney and Bud, who, with the white dogs of Brian's should catch us a pig if it hesitated long enough. So there we were zig-zagging up the hill behind Ian's house, feeling confident and lucky all at once. It was a grand day for sure and we were overdue for a pig to show for our time. Kalvin's/Brian's dogs worked all the way up the hill, mine seemed a bit more lazy, I don't know why. At the regular pig crossings they fossicked about a bit but soon lost interest. At the top of the hill we could look down on the back of a fairly big farm, the back paddock of which was a little way down the hill, with scattered gorse and tobacco-weed all along the slope. We turned right to where supposedly we might come across sign of pigs being in the vicinity. There was a track along the top which followed the fence most of the way, this fence being the divider of properties, but being in the middle of a bunch of scrub, had no battens on it. I hate having to climb over battened fences in a situation like this, as when you go to leap down the other side, there's invariably a gorse bush, or manuka stem just where your leg has to go. How much easier it is to simply spread the wires and nip through in a split second. I remember once coming to an unbattened fence, and being in a hurry, diving through the wires as I went as a dog does, and doing a forward roll on the far side, was up and on my way before the competition had even decided how to negotiate the obstacle.

About where we started to climb from a saddle, Brian's main dog began suddenly to work with a bit of purpose. Definitely more interested than before, she had her nose to the ground and was tracking over to the left, getting further into the pines and towards the same area as where Kalvin and Brian had seen the boar getting out of it the previous weekend. This looked good! Especially when Shiney began to do the same. Both white bitches sure looked business-like and we glanced at each other nodding our heads, Kalvin with his fingers crossed and me with an extra firm grip of a ti-tree stem (touching wood). We also glanced around to note what the others were up to and couldn't see a dog anywhere in the vicinity. Strange!

All remained quiet except our heart-beat – mine was hammering away inside my chest like a set of bongo drums and I took a few deep breaths to calm myself down a bit. They hadn't even found anything yet! But they did! From down towards the nearest swamp that first bark came, Brian's dog apparently. Shiney joined in almost simultaneously and a good bail was set up – and lasted no more than ten seconds. Now, ten seconds IS a good sound when heard loud and clear from 400 meres. It only becomes "un-good" when it stops, as this one did in the eleventh second. By now Kalvin and I were hurrying (not directly) down to the bail, but along the top of the ridge, hugging the fence and going in the general direction of that punch-up. We were guessing the dogs would pull their pig again further along the swamp, and sure enough they had it bailed again, still 400-500 metres beyond us, for another ten seconds. Oh no!

But yes! It all went quiet once more. Would have to be a good boar and it had two options. It would either continue on along that left-hand face and eventually run out of scrub, or cross the ridge further down from where we were and head back behind us along the river faces. If the boar knew the territory as well as I did, he'd cross over and scurry back behind us to the waterfall and somewhere beyond. Even if it continued along it still had a good chance of getting away, for the tongue of scrub was about 400 metres wide and a good kilometre long, and thick as thick at the far end. I've been onto a few pigs in there and lost them, caught others of course, and knew nothing was certain at all.

"Hey, listen!" Kalvin had his hand up and pointed with the other further down the slope and not too far ahead. "They've caught it Reg, c'mon."

"I can't hear anything; you sure?"

"Yeah, c'mon. They've definitely got it. I can hear them."

I just then saw Shiney and Tahi running away from me and angling uphill, but in a position where Kalvin couldn't catch sight of them. He was that convinced that it was all on that he was off at high speed, heading lower towards the swamp. I remained where I was, in time to see Buddy on the trail of Shiney and Tahi and couldn't make out why they would have left a definite bail like what Kalvin reckoned was in progress down his way. I stayed put a wee bit longer and listened. Not a "peep" out of his neck of the woods.

From above me though I heard a scoff, a bark, and then a squeal not any great distance away. I climbed as fast as I could go, grabbing hold of pine trees to give my legs some help and came a half-minute later to where, on the centre of the ridge, my three dogs were restraining a black boar of around eighty/ninety pounds. Not the big one. But it would be good eating and I helped the dogs win by sticking it in the prescribed manner.

Now I could hear noises from down below – Kalvin's voice.

"You get it Reg?"

"Yeah. A black boar." (he was expecting 140lb maybe).

"Yell out again; where are you?"

"Up here mate." (loudly).

Then I could see him toiling up the hill, looking my way from halfway down the slope. Most of his dogs were with him too. But even as we carried the pig out, he still insisted he had heard a good bail-up just before we caught the eighty-pounder. I was sceptical. Until after I got home.

"Hey Dad, guess what Mike and I saw this morning."

"A purple flying pussy-cat?"

"Don't be silly. Seriously, we saw a pig on the bush road. We were just walking along when it popped out thirty metres in front of us."

"You're kidding me?"

"No, eh Mike. It was black and – ."

"How big?"

"Aw, I dunno. A boar though. I've seen enough of your pigs to know

Des in typical pig country – Joe, on lookout.

it was a boar. A lot bigger than that dog." (pointing at Shiney).

Aha! Cunning old boss hog! This was just across the shallow river (ankle deep) from where Kalvin and I, at that precise time, were wondering where our boar was going to bail again. That Kalvin had heard a further thirty-second bail I didn't now doubt. The pig Angela and Mike had seen a few minutes later was our boar, having crossed the ridge like I guessed he might, and splashed through the river, run across one paddock into the bush, burst out onto the road and after growling at my hand-in-hand family, had stormed off towards Mt. Knobby – quite literally sneaking out the backdoor.

Humpty Dumpty

Every now and again a peculiar circumstance occurs to stick in your mind. This even happens in the bush while pig hunting and because of its rarity or weird character becomes a once in a lifetime experience. It happened to me recently.

On Saturday 07-07-07 I was hunting by myself in one of my regular spots. Sam Harris was possibly going to come north to join me but the weather on Thursday and Friday indicated the likelihood of it being miserable out and about. Besides he had to look after his new son according to the schedule. Jodi had plans even more important than Sam's hunting, so being the gentleman he is agreed he would occupy the hot seat.

I wasn't' too sure on Friday myself whether I'd make it either. Mentally I was all geared up in the unlikely event of more clement weather on the morrow.

And so it dawned. The wind had dropped right away, the rain had cleared up, and I was just a tad excited about a foray into the vast expanse of manuka and gorse where a pig was just bound to be waiting to tease the dogs. In fact I was going to catch a boar that had been giving Sam and I a bit of a run-around of late. On another Saturday a month or so ago he and I went looking for our friend/foe – and found him, at least Joe did. We had only just got started on our walk, intending to head up a scrub infested fenceline to the top of a high hill and then down a ridge where Kalvin Roycroft, Brian Back-house-Smith and I had distracted him a fortnight previously. Didn't get that far though. Down on our left the ground dropped away in a series of small gorse-covered flats to the stream coming from the bridge and beyond. Some beehives perched on their wooden stands alongside the manuka just in front of us and as I deliberated on which way to go around them, Kiwi, Joe and some other dogs slipped away towards the small flats. I didn't take much notice just then, but did so in a big hurry as Joe opened up really close in. Nearly 200 metres from the beehives he had put up a good pig which straightaway shortened the distance between us. Another dog joined in, enough perhaps to make the pig veer sharp left and head uphill. The odd bark was heard and we could tell where they were going easily enough and were looking over beyond the beehives. Then slightly above where we thought the pig may be we saw Shiney heading at pace up a short, more open space in the greenery. A fairly steep face here was eroded and a semi-canyon came directly towards us and it was just beside this we saw the white dog leaping uphill.

A few more stints of barking at various stages along the hill, left us with the impression we were still in with a chance. Listening and trying to figure out where best to go finally had us pelting down another boundary fence where the chase seemed to turn and head towards Skippers swamp. Stopping at intervals we ascertained from the bailing that one or more dogs had stopped the boar and were confronting it somewhere down towards that swamp. On we went, crossed a small stream, climbed among some pine trees and listened again. Silence greeted us. Blast! But Sam was off downhill. What had he heard? I'd better scarper or I'll get left behind and not benefit from his sharper ears so off I scooted in his wake.

What he had heard was a scuffle on yonder low ridge. And I heard now too, a dog getting hurt and not liking it. A couple of yelps spurred us both on and as we crossed Skipper's swamp Sam slowed and pointed up a short way, nodding his head. His progress uphill was slightly more cautious now and somewhere ahead a boar was getting quite cantankerous and I noticed Sam's gun already in his hand as he breasted the rise.

I moved up behind him. A pig track traversed the length of the low ridge and Sam moved left for about 50 metres and cocked his head on the side, shaking it with a frown on his face. He didn't remain there but came back past me and went on much the same distance. I stayed where I was to listen and watch. Next thing a dog barked and Sam's gun went off both at seemingly the same time. Gave me quite a fright, they were only a few metres away. I hadn't seen Sam aim either, was looking the other way.

He told me later that the cunning old blighter had been there all the time, Joe on guard a couple of metres away and staying uncharacteristically silent. Sam almost walked onto the boar and had only time for a hasty shot as it broke from beside him and bolted away.

Joe's bark came too at the pig's disappearance and Sam's reappearance, and he gave chase but lost it on the other side. Shiney came to us about then sporting a $300 gash in her hindquarters. Nothing life-threatening though, only Olive-threatening if she found out I'd have to give the vet some more money.

So that was our hunt for the day. Sam was kicking himself over such a good chance missed, a shot missed and a dog missed. Kiwi hadn't been in on the action at all it seemed and in fact didn't turn up until an hour or so later looking as fresh as. My mate scratched his head again, a rueful expression on his dial. It's always disappointing to be so close to success, only to fail in the end – but that's hunting. We'd try again.

And did, three weeks later. We teamed up again and had a look in the direction the boar had disappeared. Nothing was put up this time and so we crossed the river to hunt over towards Paul's place. Sam had never been here before though I had on numerous occasions and was headed for a fenceline ridge above a waterfall. The scrub hereabouts often saw pigs coming and going as was evident by the well worn path we were following. It wound in and out but ever upwards to precisely the same place Philip Foster and I nailed a good pig some years ago. Being in the area of the bone-arrow boar we had thought it may have been him, but now I tend to discard that notion. The bone-arrow boar would always run, and keep running, whereas this one stood and fought, to his downfall.

Today we arrived at the fenceline and hopped through the slack wires. Kiwi and Joe were gone somewhere and we decided to wait here in the tall ti-tree, intending to angle back and up for the return trip. I seem to remember Tahi being away too, and we had Chief, Shiney and Bud, Wiki and Joy mooching about, no doubt waiting too. Wiki had only been on five pigs so far, whereas Joy had only seen one. They were both very much learners but enjoying the outing tremendously, Wiki in particular following Bud, his father everywhere. Down below only a short distance, Sam's dogs found and let us know loud and clear. The pig they found didn't hang about, much as we would have liked him to, but took to his heels immediately and went downhill in a big circle to the right. We lost contact then and moved closer together to whisper as we continued to listen. I hadn't brought my rifle this time as I'd be with Sam throughout and was to rue my decision within the minute. Some more barking from much the same place apprised us of the fact that another pig was coming our way – and fast. I was on the up-side of the fence,

Sam ten metres below and downhill. The dogs, Jess and Tahi we.
20 metres themselves behind a great red boar that appeared, crashe.
through the fence, and went by me within almost arms length. And
stink! He hadn't had a bath for a month I'm sure and certainly didn't
use cologne. And I had an ideal chance to put a shot his way – if only I
had brought my gun. Jess was the least experienced among Sam's pack
and Tahi was a bit jaded after hunting all morning, keen-as though, but
I didn't really expect them to stop him in the absence of more resolute,
younger dogs. Sam moved up, eyes agog as I was telling him of the red.
. . . . .

"Sh, sh!" He was staring up along the fenceline and never had a
chance to explain.

Boom! I saw the gun go up an instant before the bang and swung
my gaze back to the track where the red boar had scarpered. And there
went another boar, a big black one of similar size, powering away with
no dogs on him. Joe and Kiwi turned up in about five seconds and were
encouraged along his trail but they missed too. Apparently the black one
was the original quarry and Joe and Kiwi had chased him in a big circle.
As he came down the fenceline, Sam's good ears alerted him in time to
snap that shot away but more than likely a ti-tree stem was the recipient
of the .44 bullet – more's the pity. But we do know now of two good
boars we can search for. Both would have to be 150 plus if my hasty
estimation was close. The red one just may be the bigger of the two.

Those two boars ran in a northerly direction and if they continued on
would cross the clay track and end up under the airstrip. Every now and
again a boar took up residence there, it was a sort of backwater place and
rarely got hunted. I knew about it of course but didn't often visit either.
Maybe once every two years would see me investigating its ponga and
korau slopes. Covering about 150 acres, most of the easier country has
now been put in grass and the place Philip Foster and I caught a 154lb
father pig as told on page 88 of "*The Wild Boars of Oruaiti*" was more
rye-grass than gorse now. There still was enough cover to encourage
a wild pig to stay if ever one wandered over, or was chased like these
two. And the black one could well be the nasty brute that had ripped
Shiney on her rump, and Buddy, some time back. Understandably, I was
anxious to come to grips with this fellow.

Without Sam to yarn to on the way north, I was cogitating on just
where to start my walkabout. I had been thinking of heading directly to
the clay track looking for hoof-prints to indicate he had in fact sought

refuge in the backwater 'neath the 'strip. I wasn't counting pukekos this morning as I sometimes do – didn't notice the green and white carpet of snowdrops, pretty as they were, nor yet the water temperature gauge coming up – I was miles away. I only just made it to the river before steam convinced me something was up and I had to twiddle my thumbs for half an hour while the engine cooled off enough to refill the radiator. (I'm going to get a new Hilux one day!)

My thought had convinced me however to start at Ian and Avanol's place on the off chance that one or more of those two boars had settled in well before the clay track. Had I gone directly to it I may have bypassed a good pig and an opportunity to exercise the dogs early on. Ian nearly always had news of the pig's likely whereabouts, and would tell me of their digging on his river flats or cow paddock, even close to his garden. Avanol wasn't in sympathy with the black night-time visitors having a feed of her cucumbers and tomatoes either, and agreed the pigs would have to go. Her sympathy was with them though once they were pointed away from her garden and towards the bush. The sound of a pig squealing as the dogs tormented it wasn't one of her favourite symphonies and I was at pains to have my hunting coincide with her visit to town or trip overseas. I even had a heart-to-heart chat with Rebel and co and instructed them most vehemently that they were to chase any closely-found pigs over the skyline before grabbing them. This they tried very commendably to do out of deference to Avanol's soft heart. They were even fairly successful as she hadn't yet heard any fiendish dying concert these local pigs put on when heading for the sky.

So today I left my truck just past the house, let the five dogs out, put rip-collars on and slung on my belt, rifle and gloves. If I put some string in my pouch for carrying out a pig or three, that's tempting fate and I'll miss out. If I leave string behind I'll catch one for sure. So the best thing to do is decide loudly not to take any, yet surreptitiously sneak some into my bum-bag anyway. I'd like to pass that tip on for whoever. You just never know!

As usual Wiki was glued to Bud's backside and followed him faithfully wherever he went. Tahi too was obsessed with pigs apparently and was into every crossing and runway in earnest. Shiney stayed at heel for the first half hour, but once up on top of the main ridge, put on a very good rendition of a finder and drew Joy with her all over the place. Yet there wasn't much sign and I was quite disappointed. I fully expected there to be ample evidence up here as I hadn't been this way for quite some time.

High up near the cutty-grass where a major side ridge joined, the dogs found. Tahi's bark sounded not too far below me and my rifle was in my hands pronto. Just back a hundred metres or so we had had a big bail-up years ago and I didn't want the experience repeated. A big boar had got clean away because there was no gun instantly ready – not this time! The other dogs had gone to help Tahi and it was good to hear them getting stuck in as a team. Gingerly creeping down, it became obvious their quarry was moving, assisted by several pack members. Fur flew in all directions – literally! It was a blasted possum. A couple of scratches on Wiki's snout had made him yelp as I got there but not enough I didn't think to put him off entirely.

Having left the truck at nine o'clock and hunted as far as the clay track and beyond it was now 11am and I was traversing the Goshen graves track, still pig-less but with three possums now to the dog's discredit. It was thicker going too as I left the track and dipped down to cross the creek on some tangled logs. They had once been a bridge and I pushed on looking for another track I knew of used by Peter Greenhill and I frequently in our excursions this way. The pigs were more plentiful those days. Today I still hadn't seen any recent indication of wild pigs. The very odd mark was there, old and small, and I got further despondent. I may as well call it a day and head directly for the truck.

Yet still I pushed on, reminiscing as I walked, over all the pigs I'd caught and chased hereabouts over the years. And lamented on the scarcity of something to get after. Just down there near the dam I once had to kill a milking sow in heavy gorse and I rued the day even now. I had had a long way to go and arrived too late to save the poor thing. Yet I consoled myself thinking of the other two sows I had been able to release just further around the horseshoe – two that I had recorded on video, and ended up being philosophical again. But that didn't help just now.

I was approaching another major side-ridge and recalling once seeing a large boar shoot across the track 50 metres ahead of me. Unseen by the two dogs at heel he had made good his escape, the two at-heel dogs picking up his scent but dashing along on his back trail. Useless mongrels! Thinking these sorts of "boar" thoughts had me primed good-oh for what happened now. Ten metres below the track grew a big cutty-grass bush and into this dashed Tahi, Shiney, Bud, Joy and Wiki. The whole lot. An awful shindig erupted right then, barking, yelping, crashing about and a very loud snort. And ended ? All the dogs ran back onto the track and seemed to have lost interest in a hurry. The toi-toi feathers were still shaking and my rifle, pointing straight at it, had it properly covered. I snuck up opposite and looked into the runway, dark and menacing beneath the fronds and sooled Tahi in again. In he went, about three metres and out again.

"Here Tahi, soo, soo!" And he did the same again, in and out.

"Bud! Get him soo!" and he copied Tahi. Three metres and no further would he go. Four or five times I tried but to no avail. They were simply scared of it, like me. I thought of heading in myself, but no-way. It might get me. I tried to pluck up courage, and gave it up, tried again to sool Tahi in with the same ill-effect, and raised my rifle. Dead centre of the pampas went the bullet with a very loud "bang" – but nothing happened. He may just have been an inch to either side and I cast around for something to throw at it. Several pieces of gorse wood, fairly heavy, were close by, so keeping my gun at the ready, I flung these at the bush.

Still nothing. I sidled around a bit further, always with my rifle at the ready and glanced down to see a considerable amount of possum fur floating about. So! What an idiot – and useless mongrels! What was that snort I heard then? But did I actually truly hear it? I dunno!

Uphill about 50 metres, the side ridge led away and down this went all the dogs again. This time they stayed away a quarter-hour, so I left them and headed up to the top, all this time scanning one or two yet-open places on the far slope, hoping to see a pig break across heading for the scrub on the other side of the fence. Still they stayed away, and I almost convinced myself they were on the scent of that boar that had snorted at them from the cutty-grass bush; the cutty-grass bush he had shared for a few moments with that unlucky possum. They never found him though and returned, catching up with me as I walked the "horseshoe" and back, with nothing transpiring.

By now I was pretty demoralised. Three hours with hardly a pig mark, no proper run and, at this stage four possums. Were my dogs good, but were they good! Not exactly the usual fare of a top hunter. Perhaps then I wasn't a top hunter – but I wanted to be. Maybe I wasn't even an ordinary hunter. More than likely just a hunter. Rather than bush-bash over to Neville's new road which would take me down and across two valleys, I thought, at my age I'd take the easier option of walking the track out to John and Marion's place and then head for Des' top paddock. It would end up being a bit further but there would be more opportunity of bumping into an animal because of just that. So I trudged on, head down, kicking stones for something to do. It was just such ideal weather, if only a pig would co-operate! The expanse of gorse and manuka and pines hereabouts was certainly ideal habitat for the swine. Warm temperatures and easy contour coupled with an unending choice of home territory, ought to guarantee large pig numbers you'd think. There weren't even any deep and dark, cold and clammy gorges. All around was simply the best cover and conditions available anywhere.

The long ridge I was now climbing had obviously been in grass once. It still grew underneath and between the gorse plants and on the open patches frequently seen. Rabbit turds showed up regularly now, and I had high hopes of actually bagging the big three. Possum, rabbit and donkey. There were some of those where I was headed I knew, so kept my fingers crossed (that they wouldn't find any).

Maybe I should sell the dogs, get out of hunting – retire? May as well, going by our success today. Someone might offer me $10 for the pack. Such morbid thoughts were unusual for me I knew. Always the optimist, the bright side of life always seemed to shine through and dispel the darkness in my mind, so I was at a loss to figure out why I was so gloomy; I should be singing – well – quietly, you didn't want to disturb the park did you! Or smiling anyway. At least I didn't have to carry anything out of the bush. I would have no blood or gunk seeping down my back, or sore shoulders, let alone hips come morning. Yep! Life was great. The skies were all blue, God was in heaven and I'd just come to the top of the climb, and I had no dogs.

"I'll just duck into the shade of those trees there for a leak," I thought. I ducked "into" all right, but didn't finish the last bit. All around me, in in incredible display of market-gardening, was turned over turf to a depth of 100 cm. in almost every direction for as far as I could see. And as fresh as you ever could get. I mean, the pigs, – no, boars responsible for such wanton destruction of the good turf, must right now be fleeing for their lives with my glorious go-getters grabbing at their gonads! All thoughts of relieving myself were non-existent now. I was just so relieved to find pigs did still exist in this part of the world. And yay! "Thar she blows!"

In the distance a couple of dogs had opened up and as I went to run, saw one of the pups race off to join. Another bark came about then from another quarter, only once though, and after a pause I turned again for the first one further down the long slope. Presently Wiki went by at an angle and I veered off to follow where he was headed. Probably he could hear what I couldn't now under the pines. Aha! A pig run, churned up like the motorway. Easier for me to follow now and I pushed on hurriedly. Every now and again a bark would come, seemingly slightly nearer than before and I still hadn't heard a squeal. Over a slight rise the barking was loud and clear. Not continuous – no squeal – were they holding a boar? The lever-action Rossi was primed, ready now for whatever – fifty metres to go. And a squeal. A little squeal! A piddling little squeal! Blast!

I put the gun down and moved in. Some bigger old-man gorse was where the poor little sow had got clobbered and I put her out of her misery. A broken front leg had put "paid" to any ideas I may have harbored re releasing her again, which was disappointing. Practice, or experience, such as it was, was good for the young dogs though, and I made a fuss of the two of them. They got the picture too and hung about for more. Shiney, I think was the original finder, so I congratulated her too, and for once I think she smiled. Usually rather reserved and aloof, this time she was all aglow and wagging her tail aplenty. Maybe she had noticed my former lack of zest and enthusiasm, or despondency and was saying "See, told you so!" I gave her another hug, and set to to do the gutting thing. It didn't take long, and as I set about getting string out of my bag, noticed that I was all alone again.

I wasn't surprised really. With the amount of sign I'd seen on my way to the catch, there just had to be more pigs in the vicinity somewhere, and not too far away.

"Woof, woof,woof."

"Wif, Wif."

"Bow-wow, Arf, Arf, Arf."

"Yip, Yip, Yip" – here they come again! A heavy body was accelerating fast towards me, blowing as it came, feet pounding, and snorting in anger. A boar was on it's way and only thirty metres south. I was on it's track probably – I grabbed for my loaded rifle as I saw it come around a tree ten metres off and raised it, pulling the trigger as it rocketed by at a car's length away.

Two things happened simultaneously now and all within half a split-second of me pointing the gun. There was a loud bang and an amazing metre-high cartwheeling somersault by a hundred pound black boar. He landed three metres away, pointing back the way he had come, quivering significantly and eyes flickering ominously. I was already pulling the trigger as I pointed the rifle at it's head in an effort to be 100 % sure. I pulled and pulled and suddenly realised I hadn't reloaded. Down – up – bang! With relief now I noticed he was very still, where only seven seconds before he was moving very fast indeed. I noticed too that my little dead sow was also facing the other way, and in retrospect realised I had three very vivid recollections of the last few seconds. The first was the odour, even as he came. That all-pervading boar stench was very strong for sure, and preceded him up the trail. And then at the bang, he dropped his head and ploughed into the little dead sow. That and his momentum resulted in that great whirling somersault, going head over turkey a metre off the ground. I doubt whether Humpty-Dumpty's fall was anywhere near as spectacular or dramatic as Mr. Boar's today. Certainly his was a very fast, and therefore a very great fall.

In my mind as he did that great forward roll, he weighed around 150lb – just a spontaneous fleeting impression. Not an assessment, there wasn't time, just the marking down in one's mind of a round figure "guesstimate". Whereas in truth, while he was definitely a full-grown stinking daddy pig, the scales only said ninety pounds when I weighed him the next day.

But of course! Why hadn't I thought of it! What with the delay in putting him on the scales, the hot air of the night and morning, and the wind on his body hanging in the tree – you know – dehydration and so-on, he must have lost all of forty pounds? So that means yesterday he must have weighed about 130lbs. If he had collected me instead of the bullet, I bet he would have weighed 170lbs. Have I fooled anyone?

There was one other gratifying outcome too. Tahi, Shiney, and to some lesser degree Bud, are all gun shy and took quite some time to put in an appearance. Wiki and Joy were there within seconds, not phased by the gun at all and were obviously burning up trail flat-out behind him when the gun went off. It augers well for future hunts and I'm pretty stoked!